Twayne's English Authors Series

Sylvia E. Bowman, *Editor*

INDIANA UNIVERSITY

Sir John Vanbrugh

TEAS 191

Sir John Vanbrugh
from a painting by Sir Godfrey Kneller *for the Kit-Cat Club*

SIR JOHN VANBRUGH

By ARTHUR R. HUSEBOE

Augustana College

TWAYNE PUBLISHERS

A DIVISION OF G. K. HALL & CO., BOSTON

Library of Congress Cataloging in Publication Data

Huseboe, Arthur R.   1931-
    Sir John Vanbrugh.

    (Twayne's English authors series; TEAS 191)
    Bibliography: p.163–71.
    Includes index.
    1. Vanbrugh, John, Sir, 1664–1726.
PR3738.H8   822'.4 [B]   76-18217
ISBN 0-8057-6665-0

For CARL and LILLIAN HUSEBOE
my parents

Barker, the youngest daughter of Sir Dudley Carleton of Imber Court in Surrey, had already begun to "breed like a tame rabbit," to use the lively phrase that Captain Vanbrugh employed in his first acted play, *The Relapse*. Before she had done, she was to bring fifteen more children into the world.[4] Large families were, in part, a matter of sound economy, for in plague time there was no telling how many might be taken, and there had to be a generous planting to be sure of any crop at all. In those days, older children were taught as a matter of course: "Be kind to your little brothers and sisters, for they won't be with you long." Giles Vanbrugh was more fortunate than many, for by 1683, when he wrote his will, thirteen of his children were still living, including the eldest son John.

According to the account John provided later in the pedigree required by the Heralds' College, his great-grandfather had fled from Ghent into Holland in the 1560's to escape persecution by the Duke of Alva, governor of the Spanish Netherlands. The great-grandfather's son, Giles, born in Ghent, immigrated to England about the turn of the century, "for the enjoyment of the reformed religion." Giles was nationalized in the reign of James I, received into the Anglican church, and married to an English girl named Mary, who gave birth to their second son in April 1631, in the parish of St. Stephen's Walbrook. This second son, named Giles after his father, is—of course—the father of the future comic poet and architect.

The younger Giles married late, but he chose well. His elder brother William, who had succeeded to his father's business, had already married Dorothy, the second daughter of Sir Dudley Carleton; and in early 1660 Giles took to wife the fifth daughter, Elizabeth, the co-heiress to Sir Dudley and a widow with a young daughter.[5] The Carleton family was especially fortunate in its connections, for the father of Dorothy and Elizabeth was the nephew and heir of his more famous namesake, Sir Dudley Carleton, ambassador to Holland and secretary of state under Charles I. He had been created Baron Carleton of Imber Court near Esher in Surrey (where John Vanbrugh was to build for himself many years later); and, in July 1628, he became Viscount Dorchester. The nephew, too, had participated in affairs of state as acting ambassador to Holland and as king's resident in Holland; he was appointed clerk of the council in 1637.

It may have been to Elizabeth's father's residence that she and

Giles fled with their children in the summer of 1665 to avoid the plague that had begun to ravage London. All we know for certain is that the last entry of a birth in the St. Nicholas register—that of Elizabeth—is January 7, 1665. When we hear of the family again, it has settled far to the northwest of London in the walled city of Chester where the register of Holy Trinity Church records the burial of the infant Carleton on October 13, 1667, and of little Elizabeth on November 27, 1668. The likelihood that some portion of the two-and-a-half year interim was spent with Sir Dudley is strengthened slightly by the fact that Giles and his wife chose to name the son born in 1666 after his grandfather.

Giles Vanbrugh's life as a sugar-baker in Chester seems not to have been remarkable before 1678. He went about his business, acquiring a fortune, adding children, and establishing himself as a person of note, one fit to be listed in Blome's *Britannia* in 1673 as "Giles Vanbrugh of Chester, Gent." But in 1678, when John was an impressionable fourteen years old, the news of the Popish Plot set Giles to dreaming of a way to counter the diabolical Papists to the immediate advantage of England and—certainly—to revenge himself at long last upon the religion that had persecuted his grandfather a century before. Fixed before his mind's eye, perhaps, was the English naval expedition that eighty-three years earlier had brought back the plundered libraries of Cadiz to build the great Bodleian collection at Oxford. As a result of his views, he sent an astonishing letter to the Bishop of London:[6]

The Horrid Plott Lately discovered against his Majesty, the Kingdome, and the Protestant Religion, and certainly knowne to have been hatch'd at Rome, and chiefly further'd by the Pope himself, has renewed in my thoughts, what I have often wish'd and Judg'd easily feasible. But I doubted ye proposition would have been rejected and thought a little dishonourable to attaque a prince in his owne Dominions without a just pretence or provocation.

It is, in short, my Lord, ye assaulting the City of Rome on that side where ye Vatican Palace stands, and bringing away the Library.

Giles had spent a year in Rome, he continued, and two more elsewhere in Italy and France, and knew to the last detail the size of the garrison and the time of march from the sea. Furthermore, since Sir John Nasborough was already in the Mediterranean with his fleet and with four thousand well-armed men, he might accomplish the assault on the Palace within twenty-four hours. And for good measure, Giles concluded, Nasborough might as well send eight or ten frigates to Loretto to raze the Santa Casa (reputed to have been brought from Nazareth by angels in the thirteenth century) and to carry away its costly treasures. But, though Giles offered his life and his fortune to the cause, King Charles was strangely unresponsive; and the sugar-baker lived to see the day nine years later when a Catholic king of England would visit Chester to persuade its leading citizens that the Test Act, designed to limit officeholding to loyal Anglicans, must be repealed.

An event in that latter year (1687) suggests something more about Giles's religious beliefs. In June, the well-known dissenting preacher Matthew Henry moved to Chester and was warmly received by Vanbrugh and other worthy gentlemen: "They were not altogether Strangers to Mr. *Henry* before he came to live among them, but now they came to be his very intimate Acquaintance; some of these, as Alderman *Mainwaring* and Mr. *Vanbrugh* . . . were in Communion with the Church of *England*, but they heard Mr. *Henry* on the Week-day Lectures, and always treated him with great and sincere Respect."[7] Young John was reared, therefore, in a household of ardent low-church Protestantism; and that he developed at least a distaste for its most extreme advocates is strongly hinted in his Preface to *The Relapse* in which he refers to them as "the Saints (your thorough-pac'd ones I mean, with screw'd Faces and wry Mouths)," who "love nothing, but their Altars and Themselves: they have too much Zeal to have any Charity; they make Debauches in Piety, as Sinners do in Wine; and are as quarrelsome in their Religion, as other People are in their Drink . . . ."[8]

Tradition has it that John was given a liberal education at the King's School which was highly regarded for the excellence of its instruction. It was, at any rate, the only school in Chester; and it would have provided him with his first knowledge of English drama and perhaps also of architecture. Tradition has it, furthermore, that he began his formal architectural training in France in 1683, the year—interestingly enough—in which his father made the will that left John two shares in the estate and the other children one each. But it is just as likely that John's architectural inclinations developed informally and were entirely due to his powers of observation, to his imagination, and to his good fortune in residing in a town rich in

Medieval structures. Jonathan Swift's couplet accepts the latter likelihood: "Van's genius, without thought or lecture, / Is hugely turned to architecture."[9]

II *The Grand Tour*

But, if young Vanbrugh had prepared plans for a career in building design, they were abruptly shelved when his plea to the Earl of Huntingdon late in 1685 brought an immediate and favorable response—a commission in Owen MacCarthy's company of the earl's regiment of foot.[10] The request that John sent deserves to be reprinted not only because it is his earliest extant letter but also because it is the starting point in his military career:[11]

Chester the 28th of Dec[br]: 1685

To the Rht: Hon[ble]:
The Earle of Huntington,
In Gerard street
In Gerrards buildings
London

My Lord
The favour y[r] Lordship has been already pleas'd to shew me, makes me presume that if you see it convenient y[r] Lordship will graunt my request; which is that you would please by a line or two to proffer my service to my Lord Leiuetenant of Ireland, if I may be admitted into such a station as may be at present creditable, & may have reason to expect a suitable advance, as my behaviour may prove. But if y[r] L[d]ship for reasons best knowne to y[r]self, may not thinke fitt to do what I ask. I begg your L[d]ships pardon for the trouble my presumption gives you, and am satisfied:
I humbly congratulate y[r] L[d]ship in the employ I hear the King has been lately pleased to confer upon y[o]: of Cheif Ranger: what sort of Servants y[r] L[d]ship may need to assist y[o]: in this new business, I cannot tell; but if there be any thing I am capable of, and y[r] L[d]ship thinks fitt to employ me, I should be glad of such an oppertunity by my faithfull and dilligent performance of my duty to shew that I am thankfull for the kindness I have already receiv'd:
My Lord Leiutenant has been here three days, and very respectfully treated all the time at the Castle. he is this morning gone for Holyhead, but will be four dayes e're he gett there, so probably w'on't reach Ireland till fryday or satterday.
Once more I begg y[r] L[d]ships pardon for the Trouble I give you, and subscribe my selfe as in duty bound
Y[r] Lordships most Obliedged kinsman &
faithfull Servant
John Vanbrugh

There were two arrows in Vanbrugh's bow: if the Earl of Clarendon, King James' new lord lieutenant of Ireland, had no place for him, his kinsman the Earl of Huntingdon might have. The earl's appointment as lord chief justice and justice in eyre of the royal forests south of the Trent was not effective until January 16, 1686; but he had a convenient place for a new officer in his regiment of foot (raised the previous July to help put down Monmouth's Rebellion), one quite adequate for a young man whose mother was a rather distant relative but one whom Huntingdon had already assisted. Vanbrugh's commission came through on January 30.

Within seven months, however, Vanbrugh had resigned, perhaps because he was ordered to Guernsey, perhaps because a military career did not accord with the quiet philosophic life he coveted. In a letter to Lord Carlisle thirty-five years later, Vanbrugh recalled nostalgically that from age twenty he had grown increasingly convinced that "the less one has to do, with what is call'd the World, the more quiet of mind; and the more Quiet of mind, the more Happyness."[12] At all odds, whatever his inclinations, we have nothing but the barest speculation to fill the two years from August 1686 to September 1688.

For many years, the most thoroughly documented part of John Vanbrugh's early career was his arrest and imprisonment in France—thought to have occurred during the summer of 1690—perhaps because he was caught without a passport during wartime, perhaps because he was suspected of copying down the fortification of Calais. With the recent discovery in the Public Record Office of still another early Vanbrugh letter, we can now add many details to that episode. It appears that he had been clapped in jail two years earlier, in September 1688, for associating in The Hague with supporters of William of Orange and for speaking in favor of William's planned invasion of England.[13] Vanbrugh's letter, dated August 26, 1692, is to an unknown correspondent; but it reveals the circumstance of his imprisonment as well as a remarkably humane side of his character, a side that may be inferred from the affectionate title "Brother Van" bestowed upon him by the Kit-Cat Club, but not known in such detail until now. He writes from the Bastille as follows:

Sir

Tho' I have not ye honour of being personnaly known to you; the unfortunate condition in W^{ch} I am, and have been near four years, I hope will excuse my begging Y^r assistance.

I was arrested S^r about ye time ye Warre broak out, accus'd of speaking something in favour of ye enterprize the King [William] was then upon ye point of executing upon England. And the accusation was easily believ'd, upon Mr Skeltons acquainting Mr de Louvoirs, That I had been at the Hague in my Lord Willoughbys Company; That I was his Relation, and that (as he was pleas'd to say) I lead all the Bertie family, W^{ch} way I wou'd. Upon this score, I have been us'd (till of late) with all the vigour upon earth.
. . .

In view of Giles Vanbrugh's ardent anti-Catholicism, we are not surprised that his son should have said something in favor of a Protestant prince. And, to be on friendly terms with members of the Bertie family, notorious for its anti-Popish sentiments, would further incur the displeasure of Bevil Skelton, James' envoy to Holland and France.[14] Since Skelton was imprisoned by James on September 17, 1688, for advising Louis XIV to make a military demonstration on the Dutch frontier against William, we can date Vanbrugh's arrest as shortly before then.

III *In and Out of the Bastille*

The imprisonment that Vanbrugh described in the first portion of his letter must have been at first at Calais, for a number of French references to his arrest and detention there include an order to Calais from King Louis himself that, because of the English treatment of an arrested French agent, Vanbrugh must be guarded "plus étroitment" so that he might not escape. In February 1691, the commandant was censured for allowing his English prisoner "to walk about Calais for three days." The close confinement there began to affect Vanbrugh's health; and he was moved in May 1691, at his own request, to Vincennes; and he was allowed in October to take exercise in the courtyard because a French friend had provided a sum of ten thousand francs as surety.

But, in spite of the improvement in John's situation, he wrote to his mother that same month complaining of his treatment. The letter was stopped; the king was informed; and, through his minister Pontchartrain, Louis ordered the governor of Vincennes to "supply him with all that he may need, and . . . treat him well, so that his Majesty is no longer importuned by his complaints." The complaints continued, and in February of the following year "M. de Vanbrugh, Anglais," was transferred to the Tower of Liberty in the famous Bastille where the food was good and where he was allowed to walk in the courtyard and receive visitors. And it is there that he penned the letter of August 26, 1692, explaining the circumstances of his imprisonment and continuing his efforts to obtain his freedom.

In that letter Vanbrugh proposed a solution to the problem of exchanging prisoners—a delicate negotiation that had been going on since the arrest of the French agent Bertillier early in 1691. The French had offered Vanbrugh, a Mr. Goddard, and Montague North in exchange for Bertillier; but, said Vanbrugh, the English did not consider the trade a fair one, "My Lord Nottingham thinking it a dishonour to the Nation, to be oblieg'd to give a Prisoner of State, arrested in time of Warr, for men that have been ceas'd in time of peace, contrary to what has been practis'd in England towards the French."[15] As a solution to the impasse, Vanbrugh wished the king to know that an acquaintance of his majesty, one Count Morlette, had been imprisoned in a dungeon of the Bastille for nine years because he had been accused of spying for the king before the Glorious Revolution. The count was the son of William's former undertutor, and without the king's intervention "he is sure to pass the rest of his miserable Life, in the melancholy condition he is inn."[16]

Morlette's situation was especially pathetic, said Vanbrugh, because he had been committed to life in solitary confinement, without permission "to see, speak with, or write to any body; no, not so much as his Daughter." But by some "extraordinary means," which Vanbrugh does not explain, he himself was able to communicate with the count and learn of his hopeless situation. With this added information, perhaps the king would be pleased to arrange for the release of so many gentlemen in return for "one poor Spy." It would be pleasant to learn that Vanbrugh's intercession brought the exchange of Bertillier for Morlette and that the count was freed from his long captivity, but all that we know for certain is that on Wednesday, November 22, 1692, Vanbrugh was paroled to M. l'abbé de Lagny, who supplied a thousand pistoles "in case of escape." What led M. de Lagny, described as "farmer general" in the journal of the governor of the Bastille, to intercede for the young Englishman can only be conjectured; but Vanbrugh's charm, wit, and promise as a comic dramatist must have played some part in the matter.

Not long after, Vanbrugh and Goddard reached England, unfortunately without word of their arrival in advance, and were arrested as suspected spies. They were released only after the war minister, the Earl of Nottingham, informed the mayors of Folkestone and Dover "that these gentlemen have been a long time prisoners in France and are come over upon an agreement for their exchange, so that you must discharge and set them both at liberty."[17] It may have been the impeccable French that Vanbrugh displayed on the occasion, or the Gaulish cut of the clothes supplied by the generous M. de Lagny; or it may have been the excessive zeal of some minor official that led to the reincarceration. But, whatever the reason, Vanbrugh and Goddard were abruptly put in gaol in their own homeland—hardly a welcome suitable for the Yule season.

We last hear of John Vanbrugh, before a long hiatus that ends with the writing of *The Relapse*, as auditor in 1692 for the southern division of the Duchy of Lancaster. The position may have come through the good graces of his cousin William Vanbrugh, now an official in the treasury, but it was enough for the time being. Giles Vanbrugh, who had died in July 1689, while his son was jailed in Calais, had left him—as his eldest son—a double share in the estate and had thereby made him his own master.

In *Lettres Philosophiques* (XIX) Voltaire expressed surprise that Vanbrugh's plays displayed no resentment against France, the country that had indulged him with this peculiar mark of her distinction. Yet Vanbrugh's prison experience was not entirely unpleasant, nor entirely unprofitable. It is conjectured by early biographers that he read widely in those years, especially French comedies and perhaps books on architecture. However well he may have been treated while behind walls, his real pleasure came in being able to boast about his imprisonment to his acquaintances; he could turn any conversation about the war to his advantage by mentioning—as a thing of some small interest to the company, perhaps—that he had been imprisoned in the Bastille, for four years. It was no mean distinction to have been in King William's service before the Glorious Revolution had been consummated and to have suffered for one's sovereign, and Vanbrugh made no effort to keep his suffering a secret.

The connection between him and the Bastille was certainly common knowledge when he became *the* playwright of the 1696–1697 season, and Richard Steele expected his *Tatler* readers to recognize the allusion to Vanbrugh in Number 26 (1709) in which Isaac Bickerstaff commented about an imagined letter from Louis XIV: "No, no, I remember too well how he [Louis] served an ingenious gentleman, a friend of mine, whom he locked up in the Bastille for no reason in the world, but because he was a wit, and feared he might mention him with justice in some of his writings. His way is, that all men of sense are preferred, banished, or imprisoned." In two letters to Jacob Tonson in 1719 and 1725, Vanbrugh alludes to his incarceration in a way that makes it clear that Tonson knew the story well. In the earlier of the two (July 1), Vanbrugh expresses something like a nostalgic affection for the city [Paris] of his final imprisonment: "And as to the Place you are in; I am so far from being disgusted to it, by the treatment I once met with That I think that very thing (at least the Occasion of it) has doubled a Romantick desire, of Seeing it again (IV, 112). His house at Greenwich, too, was called the Bastille; but we do not know whether he or someone else gave it that name.

The best-known offspring of Vanbrugh's confinement was the draft of a comedy. Voltaire informs us only that Vanbrugh wrote a play in the Bastille, but does not name it. Vanbrugh himself, in "A Short Vindication of *The Relapse* and *The Provok'd Wife*," describes *The Provok'd Wife* as "writ many years ago, when I was very young," and Cibber reports in his *Apology* that Vanbrugh had written the draft of *The Provok'd Wife* before *The Relapse* was produced and that some scenes were removed in order to make the final version. The frequency with which French words, phrases, and entire conversations appear in *The Provok'd Wife*, as they do not in the other original plays or even in the translations from the French, confirms the traditional assumption that this comedy was the one written in a French prison.

From his auditorship in Lancaster, Vanbrugh went in 1694 or 1695 into the military. Cibber speaks of him as an ensign at the time he met Sir Thomas Skipwith and incurred that "particular obligation" that he repaid with *The Relapse.* He served with enough distinction in the Marquis of Carmarthen's sea force to receive the latter's recommendation to Lord Berkeley, although young Carmarthen's word could not be especially valuable after the cowardly flight of his squadron from the Scilly Isles some months before when he mistook the sails of several merchant ships for the entire French fleet.[18] On December 31, 1695, Vanbrugh resigned a week old lieutenant's commission in another regiment to accept an appointment as captain in Berkeley's Marine Regiment of Foot. Quite unexpectedly he was about to step into an entirely new career.

CHAPTER 2

A Career in the Theater

I A New Playwright for a New Age

WHEN John Vanbrugh arrived in London in early 1696 on the eve of a twelve year long career in the theater, a new audience was in the making and the comedy of manners that had been the glory of King Charles' reign was already experiencing a renaissance just as lively as its spirited beginnings in the 1660's. By the last decade of the century, the audience that flocked to the London theaters had undergone a considerable democratization, in its makeup as well as in its taste. While it retained much of its fondness for comedy of all kinds—for "humours" comedy, comedy of intrigue, farce, and comedy of manners—it was also eager for dramatic variety. Simultaneously, a new mercenary spirit in the managers as well as the establishment of competing companies in 1695 was encouraging experimentation and creative dramatic activity of all sorts. As it happened, Vanbrugh was the right man for the times. Throughout the next dozen years, despite the pressures of an architectural career and the attacks of the moralists on his plays and his theater management, he would be an indispensible part of the London stage—as playwright, playhouse architect, theater manager, and opera impresario.

The forces that led to a broadened base of audience participation in the theater life of London in the 1690's were many, but certainly a principal one was the king's decided lack of interest in dramatic productions. Charles II, of course, had been the master patron in the 1660's and 1670's: the managers of the theaters were his officers, the actors were his servants, and the audience was often his coterie. When the king attended, as he frequently did, the playhouse was packed and the profits were good. He commissioned performances at Whitehall Palace as well, he gave court costumes to favored actors, and he encouraged playwrights, even suggesting plots and characters. His successor—after the troubled times under James were past—was the saturnine King William. Unlike Charles II, William had no love of the stage or of literature in general; and while his queen was fond of plays, she could also act quickly to suppress indecency or dangerous political views when they threatened to appear on stage.

As the king's support of the theater disappeared, so did that of his court. It is the consensus of most observers of the scene that in the early years of the Restoration the audience had been more exclusively upper class than it was in the 1690's and that the frequent attendance at plays of courtiers and literary men helped to elevate audience taste and to encourage a high level of performance by the actors. The playwright-critic John Dennis looked back over his long life in the theaters of London and concluded that in the reign of King Charles "several extraordinary men at Court" were responsible for determining what plays would succeed, for when "the Majority of them Declared themselves upon any new Dramatick performance, the Town fell Immediately in with them."[1] On the other hand, a different audience was in evidence during Vanbrugh's decade in the theater. Dennis believed that the social and educational level of the auditors by that time had declined significantly. There were among them, he declared, a great many uneducated younger brothers, newly rich merchants, and foreigners; and their preference was for spectacle and music rather than the good sense of legitimate drama.[2]

Nevertheless, until its slow death at the century's end, the comedy of manners enjoyed in the early 1690's a resurgence in popularity, beginning with Thomas Southerne's *The Wives Excuse* (1691), that has provided us with half the masterpieces of the Restoration era. The chief characteristics of that comedy of manners, throughout the forty years of its flourishing, were those that appealed to good sense and to the intellect and wit of the rakish young gentlemen and the eligible young belles in the audience. In the best of the comedies from Etherege to Vanbrugh the object was to present an amusing picture of attractive heroes and heroines outtalking, outwitting, and outloving the fops, fools, and villains who cluttered the stage. The playwright's central concern in such comedies was to distinguish between the truewit and the witwoud, between the "honest" man and the self-serving one, between the free-spirited heroine and the prude or the affected *précieuse*, between what a

man or a woman must be by natural law and instinct and what he or
she should be by the compulsion of social conventions. Once the
distinctions were made, rewards and punishments could be appropriately meted out; virtuous characters (with suitably virtuous names)
would win mistresses, mates, or fortunes, depending on which they
most deserved. Foolish or vicious characters (with names like Sir
Fopling Flutter, Mrs. Marwood, or Sir John Brute) would receive
appropriate punishment—loss of fortune, loss of lover, or (worst of
all) public embarrassment.

That the widely varied audience of the later Restoration period
would have trouble agreeing on what conduct should be rewarded
and what punished, however, is not difficult to understand. It was
not so much that Puritans and prudes were unable to see what the
playwrights intended as it was that the moralists disagreed with those
intentions. The high-spirited, sexually voracious, and skeptical hero
of the typical comedy of manners was for decent Puritans like the
reformer Jeremy Collier a "whoring, swearing, smutty, atheistical"
villain. The stage portrayal of the miserly citizen was seen as an
offensive caricature by those who prized thrift, industry, duty, and
piety. In large measure, to be sure, the difference between hero and
fool is merely a question of degree, but it is a question that is
difficult to resolve nonetheless, and John Vanbrugh's contributions
to comic drama did not make it any easier. The art of drawing fine
distinctions in matters of morals is easily as complex on stage as it is
in the philosopher's chamber. Thus, while all the rake-heroes of
Restoration comedy are flawed in various ways, those flaws tend to
be less obvious, less fully developed, less important than is true in
the case of the fools, fops, and villains around them. Yet the fact that
the rake was rewarded in play after play in spite of his vices was a
source of continuing dismay to the moral half of the audience in the
1690's.

From the earliest years and on, following the return of the king in
1660, the court and the acting companies had insisted publicly that a
major goal of the theater was to avoid the presentation of plays that
were profane, obscene, and otherwise scandalous, and to promote
decent, useful, and delightful instruction. But the moralists were
not misled by these pious disclaimers, and throughout the half century following the Restoration the stage was perpetually under
seige, the high point of criticism coming in 1698 with the publication of Jeremy Collier's A *Short View of the Immorality and Pro-*

faneness of the English Stage, a powerful attack against "the Mis-
behaviour of the *Stage* with respect to *Morality*, and *Religion*."[3]
Together with the ongoing efforts of the various societies for the
reformation of manners, Collier's book abruptly threw the companies and the playwrights—including John Vanbrugh—on the de-
fensive, and for the first time in forty years the decent part of the
audience appeared to emerge victorious.

Besides its slowly growing interest in drama that promoted virtue
by reforming rakes rather than by rewarding them, the audience of
the 1690's craved variety. And that craving was catered to after 1694
by two theatrical companies, in competition for the first time since
the monopoly had been established with the union of 1682. The
actors in the new company had revolted against the management of
Drury Lane because Sir Thomas Skipwith and Christopher Rich
were more interested in making money than they were in the sound
health of the plays and the players. The rebellious actors had the
wisdom and good fortune to secure a new play for the opening of
their Lincoln's Inn Fields theater in April 1705—William Congreve's highly successful *Love for Love*—and thus to establish themselves solidly as rivals to Drury Lane. The resulting competition
between the two theaters led to an outburst of creative activity—
playwriting, promotional efforts, and dramatic experimentation—
like none other during the Restoration. In the 1695–1696 season,
twenty-five new plays were produced, twice as many as the typical
number of premieres during the preceding thirty-five seasons. As
the turn of the century approached, both playhouses experimented
with changes in repertory in order to appeal to the widest possible
audience: a typical night's entertainment came to include the main
play with its prologue and epilogue; entr'acte music, dance, and
acrobatics; and an afterpiece. But the greatest change to come in the
new century was the audience's decided preference for spectacular
entertainments, in the first two decades for Italian opera and
thereafter for pantomime-farce.

The decade of Vanbrugh's greatest involvement in the theater saw
the end of attempts to establish a native English dramatic opera and
the successful introduction into England of Italian opera. Sir William Davenant had begun the genre of musical drama during the
interregnum with *The Siege of Rhodes*, and John Dryden, Henry
Purcell, and a number of other dramatists and composers had continued it. Shortly after the first Italian opera was produced in Lon-

don, however, the vogue for foreign imports caught on and many
opera performances followed. That first production, *Arsinoe, Queen
of Cyprus*, was presented by Christopher Rich in January 1705, in
the narrow confines of the Drury Lane playhouse. The opening of
the Queen's Theatre by Vanbrugh and Congreve the following
spring was a far more important encouragement to Italian opera,
however, for, despite the house's early acoustical difficulties, it was
eminently suitable for the production of spectacular entertainment
and of grand opera in particular. By early 1708 and Vanbrugh's first
season of opera in Queen's, the Italian version had effectively
supplanted serious musical drama of native growth.

II *Taking London by Storm*

With a commission fresh in his pocket, Captain John Vanbrugh went one January evening in 1696 to the Theatre Royal in
Drury Lane to see a new comedy by Colley Cibber, *Love's Last
Shift: or, The Fool in Fashion*. He was amused by the play and
impressed by its success, and he determined to write a sequel, both
to gratify an old ambition and to satisfy a new debt. To Sir Thomas
Skipwith, one of the Drury Lane managers, he owed an obligation of
some standing, although we do not know how it was incurred. According to Cibber, "When he was but an Ensign, and had a Heart
above his Income, he happen'd somewhere, at his Winter-Quarters,
upon a very slender Acquaintance with Sir *Thomas Skipwith*, to
receive a particular Obligation from him, which he had not forgot at
the Time I am speaking of. . . ."[4] Skipwith was as genial and careless about his own interests in the theater as his partner Christopher
Rich was power-hungry and incompetent.[5] Since their mismanage-
ment and their competition from the newly established playhouse in
Lincoln's Inn Fields had brought the finances of Drury Lane to a
dangerously low ebb, Vanbrugh's first play, *The Relapse* (1696),
must have been especially welcome.

There had been but one theatrical company in London between
1682 and 1695, but Christopher Rich had so antagonized the Drury
Lane actors by cutting their salaries and by giving their best roles to
beginners that a group of them under the leadership of Thomas
Betterton rebelled, "Being noe longer able to suffer & Support
themselves under the unjust oppressions and Violations of almost all
the By lawes Customes & usage that has been established among
us."[6] Betterton, then sixty and generally acknowledged as the

greatest actor of the time, obtained a license from the king and in March 1695 established a new theater at the tennis court in Lincoln's Inn Fields.[7]

Betterton's rebellion served as the object of Vanbrugh's light-hearted satire in March 1697, in which he retold the episode in the opening scene of *Aesop*, part II. In it, the rebelling actors are satirized for going against the authority of the patent. Since Skipwith liked to refer to them as "Mr. Betterton & his Mutinous Companions,"[8] Vanbrugh compares the Drury Lane company in a scene to a storm-wrecked ship that is abandoned by her crew in favor of a small bark. And, when Aesop tells the fable of the foolish hunting dogs who fled the huntsman and nearly starved, the players agree to begin peace negotiations immediately. But, in reality, negotiations were to wait for more than a decade; and, from 1695 until Vanbrugh constructed the Queen's Theatre in the Haymarket, theatergoers divided their patronage between the two companies.

The play that Captain Vanbrugh presented to Skipwith and Rich at this crucial juncture in theatrical affairs had been composed at top speed between January and early April when it was accepted by the managers.[9] But, since it was completed too late to be presented that season, it was deferred to the next. *The Relapse; or, Virtue in Danger* opened at the Theatre Royal on a particularly stormy Saturday night on November 21, 1696.[10] Lord Foppington was played by Colley Cibber, the playwright whose *Love's Last Shift* had inspired Vanbrugh.

The troupe of young actors who were given the roles in Vanbrugh's new play virtually assured its first night success and helped to establish it as a stage classic for the next century and to elevate Vanbrugh to the first rank of contemporary dramatists. Young Worthy was played by Mrs. Mary Kent, in keeping with the Restoration practice of casting women in men's roles. In thus sacrificing verisimilitude, the managers were frankly exploiting the drawing power of sex in so-called "breeches parts" that allowed a rather more generous display of the female leg than was possible in the full dresses of the day.[11] Two of the great comedians of the era had minor roles: Serringe the surgeon was portrayed by the witty Joe Haines; and Lory by Thomas Doggett, who had scored a success as Ben in Congreve's *Love for Love*. But the part of Tom Fashion's servant "suited so ill with *Dogget's* dry, and closely natural manner of acting," said Cibber later, "that upon the second Day he desir'd it might be dispos'd of to another; which the Author complying with, gave it to *Penkethman;* who though, in other Lights, much his Inferior, yet this Part he seem'd better to become."[12]

Although there were other difficulties with the actors, even at worst they contributed to the play's opening night success. George Powell, who portrayed Worthy, was envious of Cibber's gorgeous costume and "reproach'd our Master in very rude Terms, that he had not so good a Suit to play *Caesar Borgia* in! tho' he knew, at the same time, my Lord *Foppington* fill'd the House, when his bouncing *Borgia* would do little more than pay Fiddles, and Candles to it. . . ."[13] Powell might well have been annoyed, for Cibber had developed the dressing scene into an outrageously funny piece of stage business. The periwig alone, as Pope recounted later, was so elaborate that it "made its entrance upon the stage in a sedan, brought in by two chairmen, with infinite approbation of the audience."[14]

A further difficulty with Powell occurred on opening night. In the preface to the printed edition of *The Relapse,* Vanbrugh described the event: "The fine Gentleman of the Play, drinking his Mistress's Health in *Nants* Brandy, from six in the Morning to the time he wadled on upon the Stage in the Evening, had toasted himself up, to such a pitch of Vigor, I confess I once gave *Amanda* for gone. . ." (I, 12). The audience was delighted. Powell's vigorous attack suited well the new, more realistic mode of acting developed by the company, and Vanbrugh's new comedy—praised by the actors for the easy flow of its lines[15]—was the perfect vehicle for them.

The scene on that opening night and each night of the following week can only be conjectured, but a lively and amusing description of a visit to the Theatre Royal in the following year has been preserved in Henri Misson's *Memoirs:*

The Pit is an Amphitheater, fill'd with Benches without Backboards, and adorn'd and cover'd with green Cloth. Men of Quality, particularly the younger Sort, some Ladies of Reputation and Vertue, and abundance of Damsels that hunt for Prey, sit all together in this Place, Higgledy-piggledy, chatter, toy, play, hear, hear not. Farther up, against the Wall, under the first Gallery, and just opposite to the Stage, rises another Amphitheater, which is taken up by persons of the best Quality, among whom are generally very few Men. The Galleries, whereof there are only two Rows, are fill'd with none but ordinary People, particularly the Upper one.[16]

The "higgledy-piggledy" audience at *The Relapse* had been led to expect a sequel to Cibber's play about the reformation of a rake, but they could not have expected a triumph. Colley Cibber was magnificent as his own character, Sir Novelty Fashion, now raised to the peerage as Lord Foppington. George Powell added spice to the opening night and to successive performances; and the rest of the actors—usually acknowledged to be inferior to Betterton's troupe—rose to the occasion. The scenes closed upon Act V "with mighty applause," said Charles Gildon,[17] and from then on *The Relapse* was an important piece in the repertory. The anonymous author of *A Comparison Between the Two Stages* included it among the masterpieces upon which Drury Lane subsisted in its first two or three years, and the play remained the sole property of the Theatre Royal company until 1733.[18]

III   *Written in France*

The warm reception given *The Relapse* by the patentees in the spring of 1696 had encouraged Vanbrugh to dust off his Bastille comedy and prepare it for the stage. About the same time he began looking over with an eye to adaptation some of the comedies he had read and heard of while in prison. One of those that especially appealed to him was Édme Boursault's *Les Fables d'Ésope*, acted with success at the Comédie Française in January 1690. When the stage triumph of *The Relapse* seemed assured, the two patentees agreed that the adaptation of Boursault's episodic comedy might bring back the audience who had flocked to see the new playwright's first production. And so, in December, while the company struggled with an elaborate production of Thomas D'Urfey's opera *Cinthia and Endimion*, intended to have been performed at court two years before, Vanbrugh's *Aesop* was rushed into rehearsal. When D'Urfey's opera was damned (if it *had* been played at court, people said, it might have been blamed for the queen's death),[19] *Aesop* was brought on stage.

Despite a singular lack of success at Drury Lane, *Aesop* remained a staple in the repertory for two or three years, with Vanbrugh adding a second part some time in March; and in years to come scenes from it were played as afterpieces or as entr'acte entertainments. In addition, it began the vogue of the satiric allegory on the stage—the form used by David Garrick in his first play, *Lethe: or*

Esop in the Shades (1740)—and it also helped to popularize the anthologies of satirical fables that swarmed the book stalls around 1698, such as *Aesop at Bath, Aesop at Epsom,* and (in 1703) a collection by Bernard Mandeville, *Some Fables after . . . la Fontaine,* the forerunner of the most famous eighteenth century collection of all, *The Fable of the Bees.*[20]

His debt to Sir Thomas Skipwith discharged with the performance of *Aesop,* Vanbrugh turned the next comedy over to Betterton's company at Lincoln's Inn Fields. Cibber reported in the *Apology* that the Earl of Halifax had heard *The Provok'd Wife* read to him before *The Relapse* scored its stage success; and, when it became clear that Vanbrugh's first play had won an audience, Halifax had urged him to give his Bastille comedy to Betterton.[21] Skipwith did not object, and so the new play went to Lincoln's Inn Fields early in the new year (1697) as Vanbrugh's gift to the players. Halifax's friendship may have been his only motive, but he may also have wished to score triumphs at both playhouses so as to complete his conquest of the theatrical world, and he may have wanted to secure his reputation as an open-handed gentleman playwright rather than as the hireling of a single company. After all, Congreve had given his first play to the united company in the fall of 1693 and then had opened Betterton's new playhouse in late April 1695 with *Love for Love,* a comedy so warmly received that—as Cibber said—"they had seldom occasion to act any other Play, 'till the End of the Season." To Vanbrugh, it must have been gratifying to follow Congreve's model; but to do so with less than a five month separation between one's masterpieces must have been quite heady indeed.

The theater in which *The Provok'd Wife* had its premiere in mid-April had been remodelled from the indoor tennis court in Portugal Street that had served Sir William Davenant and the Duke's Company as a playhouse from 1661 to 1671 and Thomas Killigrew and the King's Company from 1672 to 1674 when again it became a tennis court.[22] With a number of "people of quality" subscribing to the remodelling project, the conversion was completed quickly. In spite of its small size and its inadequate stage machinery, "Betterton's Booth," as it was sometimes contemptuously called, was more popular in its early months of existence than the older playhouse, and it continued in operation until late 1705 when the Queen's Theatre in the Haymarket finally took its place. The success of *The Provok'd Wife* was a long-lasting one; for the next

three or four years it was one of the staples—along with Congreve's
The Mourning Bride and Edward Ravenscroft's *The Anatomist*—at
Lincoln's Inn Fields.[23] It was given prominent attention along with
The Relapse in Jeremy Collier's attack on the stage in April 1698;
and in November 1701 its popularity was attested to by the fact that
twelve actors—including Anne Bracegirdle, John Verbruggen, Betterton, and Elizabeth Barry—were charged with "using indecent
expressions" in several plays, especially in *The Provok'd Wife*, and
the latter two were fined.[24] With this comedy Vanbrugh made his
final contribution of an original play; for, henceforth, everything to
bear his name or to be assigned to him was to be an adaptation or a
translation. The only exception was Vanbrugh's uncompleted *A
Journey to London* which was finished after his death by Colley
Cibber and successfully staged in 1728.

With three comedies regularly on the boards, Captain Vanbrugh
was prevailed upon by Sir Thomas Skipwith to try his hand at a
fourth. Once again, he turned to the French plays with which he
was familiar; and he selected one that he may have seen in Paris
before his imprisonment. The comedy he chose to adapt was
Florent-Carton Dancourt's one act farce *La Maison de Campagne*
which had been performed first at the Comédie Française on
January 27, 1688. Neither the translation of *The Country House* nor
the performance of it claimed much of Vanbrugh's attention, for the
printed play did not appear until 1715 and then without a preface, a
prologue, or an epilogue. The play's reception was so poor that the
performance in January 1698 of *The Country House* would not be
known were it not for Professor Leslie Hotson's discovery of the
records kept by Lady Penelope Morley of her attendance at various
plays from 1696 to 1701.[25] The brevity of *The Country House* made
it suitable as an afterpiece; and, during the first half of the
eighteenth century, it was frequently presented with another play,
on eight occasions linked with the presentation of a comedy by
Vanbrugh.

IV *Troubled Playhouses*

Having brought four plays to the stage in fourteen months and
having elevated himself, with his left hand as it were, into the front
rank of English comic dramatists by setting out to discharge a gentlemanly debt, Captain Vanbrugh might have anticipated a pleasant
career as a peacetime officer who would enjoy long stays in London

and the frequent companionship of wits and great men in whose company (respectively) he might engage in high-flying wit-combats and from whom he might obtain a vacant household or a government post at three or four hundred pounds a year. But, abruptly, in April 1698, Vanbrugh was sent scrambling in an attempt to rescue both his dramatic and his military careers. About that time Lord Berkeley's Regiment of Foot was disbanded, leaving Vanbrugh with over £128. owed him.[26] And on April 16, the first of a series of advertisements appeared that announced the publication by Jeremy Collier of *A Short View of the Immorality and Profaneness of the English Stage*, a work that had a long chapter devoted entirely to Vanbrugh's *The Relapse* and that contained pot shots at him elsewhere.

When the *Short View* reached the bookstalls, it was apparent from the virulence and extent of Collier's attack on Vanbrugh that the nonjuring priest had a special score to settle with the playwright—one beyond the two popular comedies Vanbrugh had contributed to the dramatic repertory of London.[27] The problem was that in both of them Vanbrugh had baited the reforming moralists of London, and had virtually dared them to respond. The preface to *The Relapse* had ridiculed "Saints" with "screw'd Faces and wry Mouths" who "make Debauches in Piety, as Sinners do in their Wine; and are as quarrelsome in their Religion, as other people are in their Drink: so I hope nobody will mind what they say." Moreover, the Preface also contained a mock recantation and a suggestion that the printed play belonged on the same shelf as a prayer book. The Prologue to *The Provok'd Wife* had gone even farther and had invited attack:

> Since 'tis the Intent and Business of the Stage,
> To Copy out the Follies of the Age;
> To hold to every Man a Faithful Glass,
> And shew him of what Species he's an Ass:
> I hope the next that teaches in the School,
> Will shew our Author he's a scribbling Fool.
> And that the Satyr may be sure to Bite,
> Kind Heav'n! Inspire some venom'd Priest to Write, . . .
> (I, 113)

The "venomed priest" who chose to condemn the immorality and profaneness of the stage was a nonjuring, high-church priest and professional polemist who had produced a long series of pro-Jacobite pamphlets between 1688 and 1697. Collier, moreover, had been imprisoned twice for his efforts in behalf of James; and he had been declared an outlaw and condemned to death in 1696 for giving absolution on the scaffold to Sir John Friend and Sir William Perkins who were executed for their implication in the "Assassination Plot."[28] He was, as a consequence, ideally suited for the rough and tumble of a pamphlet war, and the lively style of his three hundred page attack and his refusal to be awed by the great names that he belabored brought the *Short View* an immediate success. The seven months that followed saw two more editions of the work and some eighteen pamphlet replies that were both for and against Collier's position; and these works included Vanbrugh's "A Short Vindication" and Congreve's "Amendments of Mr. Collier's False and Imperfect Citations."

Within three weeks of the appearance of the *Short View*, Narcissus Luttrell recorded on May 10 that "The justices of Middlesex did not only present the playhouse, but also Mr. Congreve, for writing the *Double Dealer;* Durfey, for *Don Quixote;* and Tonson and Briscoe, booksellers, for printing them: and that women frequenting the playhouses in masks tended much to debauchery and immorality."[29] Collier's encouragement to the moralizers posed as grave a threat to acted plays as it did to printed ones. The anonymous author of *The Laureat* (1740) remembered "that soon after the publication of Collier's book, several informations were brought against the players, at the instance and at the expense of the Society for the Reformation of Manners, for immoral words and expressions, *contra bonos mores,* uttered on the stage. Several informers were placed in the pit, and other parts of the house, to note down the words spoke, and by whom, to be able to swear to them. . . ."[30]

Vanbrugh referred to such activities in early 1702 in the Prologue to *The False Friend:* "Your Scouts indeed, sometimes come stealing in, / T'observe this Formidable Camp of Sin . . ." (II, 156). A number of arrests and trials grew out of the activities of the Society for the Reformation of Manners, some of them summarized by Joseph Wood Krutch,[31] until an edict by Queen Anne on January 17, 1704, ended their interference; but, as the arrests had multiplied, Collier had been welcomed as a great reformer. King William too was pleased at this moral turn of events; he pardoned Collier for

having absolved Friend and Perkins, even though the priest had
refused to pledge his allegiance to William.[32]

No clear evidence exists that Vanbrugh's comedies suffered an
immediate eclipse because of Collier. We have little information
about the stage histories of most Restoration and eighteenth century
plays until after 1702, when advertisements began to appear regularly in the *Daily Courant*. The only recorded performances of *The
Relapse* after Collier's attack are one in each year 1700 through
1702; *The Provok'd Wife*, on the other hand, is not listed again in
performance until January 1706. It is certain, however, in spite of
what Cibber said, that Vanbrugh knew his reputation as a wit was at
stake and that the theater itself was in danger; for Collier had made a
case in his sixth chapter for the permanent closing of all theaters. As
a result, Vanbrugh completed in six weeks and sent to the press his
seventy nine page defense, "A Short Vindication of *The Relapse* and
The Provok'd Wife, from Immorality and Prophaneness."

The weaknesses in Collier's position were readily apparent, and
Vanbrugh exploited them. The reforming divine had more than
anything else displayed an almost psychotic sensitivity to oaths and
doubles entendres; and he had dug so diligently for the least trace of
salaciousness that Vanbrugh exclaimed in disgust that "I suppose it
may be owing to the Number of Bawdy Plays he has read, which
have debauch'd his Taste, and made every thing seem Salt, that
comes in his way" (I, 196). Collier had brought his heaviest artillery
to bear against some of the most innocuous lines, said Vanbrugh,
and he had mixed literary criticism and moralizing; Vanbrugh could
easily defend the first as expressions used in the politest society, and
the fallacies inherent in the second were self-evident. Collier, in
arguing that the clergy should be portrayed in ideal terms—like
Chaucer's Parson, pure, devout, and dedicated—showed both his
reliance upon Thomas Rymer's theory of decorum (the insistence
that characters should be consistent to type) and his supersensitivity
to criticism of the cloth he wore. As Vanbrugh pointed out, however, such men as Chaplain Bull in *The Relapse* do exist; but he also
added that "what Quarrel we have to our Clergy here, points more
at the Conduct of *some,* than the Establishment of the whole" (I,
205) (italics added) and that "A Clergyman is not in any Countrey
exempted from the Gallows" (I, 208). In short, Vanbrugh's portrayal
of Bull in his play was not false; it was so dangerously true that it
brought forth Collier's barrage.

The question of morality in Restoration comedy, including Collier's chief objections, is a complex one. It is enough to say here that Vanbrugh exaggerated his moral intent in writing *The Relapse* and *The Provok'd Wife* and that Collier overreached himself in seeking immorality and profaneness. Arguments can be found to support both sides, for in matters of morals even doctors disagree. The comic actor Joe Haines (who had played Serringe in *The Relapse*) was once asked, "What could transport Mr. *Collier* into so blind a Zeal, for a general Suppression of the Stage, when only some particular Authors had abus'd it; whereas the Stage, he could not but know, was generally allow'd, when rightly conducted, to be a delightful Method of mending our Morals? For that Reason, (*reply'd* Haines:) *Collier* is, by Profession, a Moralmender himself, and two of Trade, you know, can never agree."[33] Vanbrugh himself saw the humor in two moralists quarreling about means to the same end, and he closed the "Vindication" with this witticism: "This methinks is something so very extraordinary in a Clergyman, that I almost fancy when He and I are fast asleep in our Graves, those who shall read what we both have produc'd, will be apt to conclude there's a Mistake in the Tradition about the Authors; and that 'twas the Reforming Divine writ the Play, and the Scandalous Poet the Remarks upon't" (I, 215).

V *The Theater and the Kit-Cats*

Captain Vanbrugh's career in the theater now entered a long period in which his involvement in the affairs of the two companies was only occasional. Nevertheless, the importance of his contributions to comic drama had been firmly established by the time of the Collier Controversy; his had proven to be one of the most successful defenses of the stage; and the friendships he had made with Skipwith and Rich at Drury Lane and with Betterton at Lincoln's Inn Fields and with the actors of both companies, and the close ties that adversity had formed between Vanbrugh and his beleaguered fellow dramatists combined to keep at least a part of his interest directed toward the storm center that was the London stage.

In the season of 1698–1699 that followed, the two companies continued their competition for the playgoing public by responding to an increasing fondness for music and spectacle: they produced operas and added foreign singers and dancers to the regular offerings.[34] The year, however, was not a financial success, nor was the

1699–1700 season that followed, although Rich and Skipwith gained
a comparative triumph with George Farquhar's *The Constant
Couple,* and scored what later proved to be a coup when Farquhar
introduced Vanbrugh to Anne Oldfield and when Vanbrugh rec-
ommended her to Rich. Betterton in turn had hoped to raise his
declining fortunes with Congreve's *The Way of the World.* On
Christmas day, 1699, Vanbrugh wrote to the Earl of Manchester
about the Lincoln's Inn Fields company: "Matters running very low
with 'em this Winter; if Congreve's Play don't help 'em they are
undone. 'tis a Comedy and will be play'd about Six weeks hence.
nobody has seen it yet" (IV, 4). When they did see it, however, on
March 5, 1700, it was coolly received; and it was repeated only four
more times that season.

The circle of friends in which Vanbrugh was moving in late 1699
included some of the most illustrious lords, men of letters, and
politicians of the day. And from that association was to grow his next
theatrical venture, an alteration of Fletcher's *The Pilgrim* for the
benefit of the aged and the ill John Dryden. Whether Vanbrugh was
by then a member of the celebrated Kit-Cat Club is not certain, but
he was already acquainted with men who were its members or who
were to join it later, and the club was already lending its support
early in 1700 to the theaters in which Vanbrugh had been so much
involved. On January 19, 1700, for example, Matthew Prior wrote to
Abraham Stanyan: "To-morrow night Batterton [*sic*] acts Falstaff,
and to encourage that poor house the Kit Katters have taken one
side-box, and the Knights of the Toast have taken the other."[35] The
Kit-Cat Club's frequent presence as a group thereafter is clearly
indicated by an anonymous broadside poem, "The Patentee," of
May 1700. On May 13 the two patent theaters had closed their doors
in honor of Dryden's funeral. The Dorset Garden Theatre, however, which specialized in miscellaneous entertainments, featured
bear-baiting on that day; and the poet expressed his dismay at seeing butchers and bailiffs sitting "Where Ladies Eyes were Instru-
ments to kill, / Where *Kit-Cats* sate, and Toasters would be
seen, . . ."[36]

The Kit-Cat Club in which Vanbrugh was early involved must
have originated some time before 1697, the year that eight year old
Mary, the daughter of the Earl of Kingston and later the witty and
famous Lady Mary Wortley Montagu, was proposed as the club's

toast. According to Lady Louisa Stuart's account of her grand-mother,

One day at a meeting to choose toasts for a year, a whim seized him [Lord Kingston] to nominate her . . . a candidate, alleging that she was far pret-tier than any lady on their list. The other members demurred, because the rules of the Club forbade them to elect a beauty whom they had never seen. "Then you shall see her," cried he; and in the gaiety of the moment sent orders home to have her finely dressed, and brought to him at the Tavern, where she was received with acclamations, her health drunk by everyone present, and her name engraved upon a drinking-glass. The company con-sisting of some of the most eminent men in England, she went from the lap of one poet, patriot, or statesman to the arms of another, was feasted with sweetmeats, overwhelmed with caresses, and what perhaps pleased her better than either, heard her wit and beauty loudly extolled on every side.[37]

Lady Stuart's anecdote suggests that the club had been in existence before Lady Mary's nomination as toast. John Oldmixon, as a matter of fact, states that it began just before the Glorious Revolution, when John Somers (later Baron Sommers and lord chancellor), bookseller Jacob Tonson, and another lawyer met frequently at a tavern near Temple Bar.[38]

In the early years of the Kit-Cat Club, the members had no other purpose in meeting than the pleasure of one another's conversation and of Christopher Cat's excellent meat pies. Cat, or Catling, kept a tavern at the sign of the cat and the fiddle (an allusion to his nickname Kit Cat) in Shire Lane near Temple Bar. Tonson, of course, had ulterior motives in bringing together the wits and lead-ing politicians of England at Cat's tavern. As the club's secretary, a humble position that enabled him to perpetuate its activities, he could help its men of letters find patrons among the Whig lords; he could aid the statesmen in their political wars by introducing them to the ablest writers of the day; and he could always find oppor-tunities for advancing his business by having the first look at works in progress. As the Kit-Cat Club developed into an organization with regular meetings, it assumed a more and more political cast; it established the annual ballot for the "happy virgin" who would reign as the toast for the year, her virtues celebrated in lines inscribed on the club's wine glasses; it increased its membership from the origi-nal thirty-nine to forty-eight; and it became increasingly involved in

theatrical affairs, its interest reaching a climax in the construction of
the Queen's Theatre in the Haymarket.

Among the early members of the Kit-Cat Club were many of
Vanbrugh's acquaintance. One of the least illustrious, to be sure,
was Captain John Tidcombe (later a lieutenant-general), but Vanbrugh had known him longest; for both had served in 1686 in the
Earl of Huntingdon's Regiment of Foot.[39] Congreve was, of course,
the most famous of the men of letters as the associate and literary
heir of Dryden, and Vanbrugh must have known him from the days
when *The Relapse* was the talk of London. Lord Dorset, one of the
founders of the Kit-Cat, would also have been an early acquaintance. As lord chamberlain, Dorset had helped Betterton escape to
Lincoln's Inn Fields; and his kindnesses to deserving authors had
earned him the epithet "the grace of courts and the muses' pride."
Vanbrugh's Christmas letter to the Earl of Manchester in 1699 reveals a long friendship with that ambassador extraordinary to the
court of France; and in it Vanbrugh refers to his design of Castle
Howard for the young Earl of Carlisle, to a dinner engagement with
Charles Montagu—treasurer, patron of Dryden, and later Baron
Halifax—and to Lord Carberry, one of Dryden's earliest patrons,[40]
who "toasts [Lady Manchester] with an Exemplary Constancy" (IV,
5).

John Dryden, certainly, was the most distinguished literary
member of the Kit-Cat before the seventeenth century ended. According to the *Dictionary of National Biography,* as early as 1698 Sir
Godfrey Kneller had painted the Kit-Cat portrait of Dryden at Tonson's request; and the great poet was on a familiar footing with most
of London's literary men and with a great many of England's patrons
of letters. Although Tonson was his publisher, the two men were not
always on the best of terms. Dryden's famous translation of Virgil
appeared under Tonson's imprint, as did *The Fables;* the two men
were in frequent correspondence and conversation; but on one occasion Dryden, frustrated by Tonson's dealings, wrote three lines as
a warning of the power that his pen could wield: "With leering
looks, bull-faced and freckled fair; / With two left legs and Judas-
coloured hair, / And frowsy pores, that taint the ambient air."
Among Vanbrugh's known acquaintances in the Kit-Cat Club were
some of Dryden's closest friends. Congreve, of course, was an intimate of the old poet from at least 1693 when Dryden called Congreve's *The Old Batchelor* the best first play he had ever seen. Lord

Dorset was one of Dryden's most loyal patrons; Lord Carberry, one of his earliest; and Charles Montagu, a later patron, proposed the elaborate private funeral for Dryden that never occurred. As is seen in Dryden's last letters, his final illness increased in severity during 1699; and, as an honor to the dying poet and as an advantage to his purse, Vanbrugh and the patentees of Drury Lane agreed upon a benefit production of Fletcher's *The Pilgrim* which was altered into prose by Vanbrugh. Dryden added a vigorous prologue and epilogue and a brilliant masque and Daniel Purcell and Gottfried Finger composed the music. The old poet's final letter, on April 11, 1700, to his cousin Mrs. Elizabeth Steward announces the performance as imminent: "Within this moneth there will be playd for my profit, an old play of Fletchers, called the Pilgrim, corrected by my good friend Mr. Vanbrook; to which I have added A New Masque, & am to write a New Prologue & Epilogue."[41] The benefit of the play went, however, to Dryden's son; for the old man died on May 1, 1700, the third night of the production.[42]

Why Vanbrugh chose *The Pilgrim* for the Dryden benefit is not known; perhaps Skipwith and Rich, who felt an older play was needed to counter the successful revivals of Shakespeare's plays by Betterton's company, suggested Fletcher's work. Perhaps the conversion of Roderigo from villainy to virtue—so like that of Worthy in *The Relapse* and Heartfree in *The Provok'd Wife*—appealed to Vanbrugh. *The Pilgrim* was, at any rate, a fortunate choice; for Vanbrugh's modernization, Dryden's contributions, and an outstanding performance by Anne Oldfield as Alinda gave it an immediate success.

The benefit production of *The Pilgrim* was not a Kit-Cat affair: no other members of the club than Vanbrugh and Dryden were prominent in bringing the play to the stage; and the printed version was not given to Jacob Tonson but to his fellow bookseller Benjamin Tooke. The benefit was, instead, one of Vanbrugh's remarkable acts of generosity and kindness which made the heroic epithet "Brother Van" inevitable. Not only were the profits of the third day turned over to Dryden's son, but Vanbrugh so respected the name of Fletcher and the honor of Dryden that he omitted his own name from the title page of the printed play in June, did not include *The Pilgrim* in Tonson's 1719 edition of his *Works*, and kept his name from appearing in the playhouse advertisements in spite of the fact that *The Pilgrim* was by far the most often played of all the adaptations during Vanbrugh's lifetime. With seventy-one performances, it outnumbered *The Provok'd Wife* (50), and it rivalled *The Relapse* (74)—Vanbrugh's two original plays.

Dryden's death, on the other hand, seems to have been the event that brought the Kit-Cat Club to its determination to support the declining theaters. First, his decease led to the club members' decision to provide an elaborate funeral for their late associate. According to a letter of Tuesday, May 14, 1700, sent from one Edward Hinton to the Reverend John Cooper on the day after the funeral, "Dryden was buried by the Bishop of Rochester at the Abbey on Monday; . . . the Kit-Cat Club were at the charge of his funeral, which was not great, and . . . Mr. Montague had engaged to build him a fine monument."[43] The body of the poet had been embalmed; and, because of Dr. Garth's application, it was placed in the College of Physicians until May 13.[44] From Hinton's letter we know that Garth pronounced a Latin oration on that day, and other contemporary accounts indicate that Montagu and Tonson participated in the obsequies, and that Kit-Cats were prominently in attendance. Second, Dryden's death removed from their midst the one member whose religious beliefs had made him the center of a virulent controversy. Henceforth the Kit-Cat Club would be solidly Whig and thoroughly Protestant (or at least atheistically neutral).

Early in the winter of 1701-1702, when the weather had brought a halt to the construction of Castle Howard, Vanbrugh employed a part of his enforced leisure in the translation of still another play—*The False Friend*—for the Drury Lane company. This time it was a melodramatic love intrigue that had appeared first as *La Traicion Busca el Castigo* (1640) by the Spaniard Francisco de Rojas Zorilla and that had then been adapted by Alain René Lesage as *Le Traître Puni* and printed at The Hague in 1700. Dobrée speculates that Tonson brought the Lesage play back from one of his frequent visits there, for Vanbrugh's Spanish seems to have been negligible.[45]

The Kit-Cat Club no doubt gave its full support to the play, for by this time they were attending the theaters as a group. Tom Brown in that year described a typical gathering: "L[ord] D[orset] is known by his Ribbon, and T[om] D ['Urfey] or some other Impertinent Poet, talking Nonsense to him, the L[ord] H[alifax] by sitting on the *Kitcat* side, and *Jacob* T[onson] standing Door-Keeper for him."[46] But *The False Friend* was only mildly successful, running in February for four nights before an injury to Cibber (portraying Don John) brought it to a close.

VI *A New Playhouse in the Haymarket*

By the next year (1702), the Kit-Cat Club had decided upon a project to rescue the London stage from its current state of decline by building a modern theater that would replace Betterton's booth, where the best of plays could be produced and where one could outdo even Rich in spectacles and musical entertainments. Because of Vanbrugh's success in the design of Castle Howard for the Earl of Carlisle, begun the preceding spring, and through the influence of his political friends, he had resigned another commission as captain in order to accept the position of comptroller of the Board of Works in June 1702. This appointment, as a subordinate crown architect under Sir Christopher Wren, put Vanbrugh into close contact with the center of the vast English building industry and hence into an advantageous position for obtaining land and materials for a new playhouse.[47]

The remarkable combination in Vanbrugh of playwright and architect that had brought him his unique reputation impressed the Kit-Catters as well, and from their conversations about the strange decline of the stage came the scheme for a new theater. If Vanbrugh did not make the proposal himself, he was certainly its most ardent advocate; for his letters to Tonson in the summer of 1703 indicate how completely he had made the project his own. By June 15, he says, the site has been purchased; the tenants are due to vacate by the June 21; and he has every expectation of completing the building by Christmas. In his letter of July 13, he is even more optimistic about the scheme; for it now appears that, despite the high cost of land, he would be "reimburs'd every penny of it" by the rent from the buildings on the site.

Legal problems, however, quickly beset him.[48] He first acquired the old Phoenix Inn Yard and adjacent buildings from William Wooley, "citizen and haberdasher." But, when it appeared that the ground was not large enough for the theater he had planned, he entered into a provisional agreement to purchase the necessary buildings fronting on the Haymarket from Thomas Holford, "citizen and baker." On August 14, 1703, Vanbrugh filed a bill against Holford that claimed that the owner was demanding exorbitant terms.

Holford replied in October; and in June 1704, when construction was already underway, he filed a countersuit. The settlement, in September, gave Vanbrugh ownership of valuable houses, the rent from which was to provide him with income for the rest of his life.

Legal entanglements, then, and other affairs—including the work at Castle Howard and his appointment to the obsolete post of Carlisle Herald Extraordinary on June 21, 1703—prevented work on the theater from getting underway until the following spring. The Kit-Cat Club members had promised to underwrite the cost of construction in return for the privilege for life of attending public performances; and, according to Cibber, "thirty persons of quality" eventually subscribed thirty guineas each to the project.[49] The cornerstone was laid jointly on April 18, 1704, by Lady Sunderland, the seventeen year old daughter of the Duke of Marlborough, and by the Duke of Somerset, a handsome favorite of Queen Anne and a prominent Kit-Cat.

An account in *The Rehearsal of Observator* for May 5–12, 1705, reported that "The KIT–KAT Club is now grown Notorious all over the Kingdom, And they have Built a Temple for their Dagon, the new Play-House in the Hay-Market. The Foundation was laid with great Solemnity, by a Noble Babe of Grace. And over or under the Foundation Stone is a Plate of Silver, on which is Graven Kit Cat on the one side, and Little Whigg on the other." Cibber explains that the "Little Whigg" was "a Lady of extraordinary Beauty, then the celebrated Toast, and Pride of that Party";[50] and a poem in another contemporary journal, "On the Lady Sunderland's laying the first Stone," identifies the lady.[51] Somerset's part in the ceremony is indicated by an inscription on the cornerstone uncovered when the theater was being repaired in 1825: "This corner-stone of the Queen's Theatre was laid by his Grace Charles Duke of Somerset."[52] Apparently, Somerset laid the stone; Lady Sunderland, the silver plate.

During the winter of 1704 and prior to the corner stone laying, four of the Kit-Cat Club had decided on an interim project that would assist Betterton's company, which was suffering from a gradual decline in attendance. Vanbrugh, Congreve, and William Walsh agreed each to translate an act of Molière's farce *Monsieur de Pourceaugnac* (which they named *Squire Trelooby*); and Dr. Garth was to provide the prologue.[53] Congreve explained the circumstances of the collaboration to his friend Joseph Keally in May:

The translation you speak of [*Squire Trelooby*] is not altogether mine; for Vanbrugh and Walsh had a part in it. Each did an act of a French farce. Mine, and I believe theirs, was done in two mornings; so there can be no great matter in it. It was a compliment made to the people of quality at their subscription music, without any design to have it acted or printed farther. It made people laugh; and somebody thought it worth his while to translate it again, and print it as it was acted: but if you meet such a thing, I assure you it was none of ours; which I don't think will appear again after next week, when our neighbour [Anne Oldfield] is to have it acted for her benefit.[54]

Since, as Congreve says, the Kit-Cat *Squire Trelooby* was not printed and since no manuscript form exists it may seem fruitless to speculate about which author translated which act. If we can trust "Tryall of Skill; or a New Sessions of the Poets" (1704), Congreve took the first act, but there is only the slightest evidence of Vanbrugh's and Walsh's share.[55]

Congreve's letter has, however, caused no little difficulty; for, if somebody had translated the play again, why should Congreve speak of that second translation as printed "as it was acted"? The second translation, advertised in *The Daily Courant* for April 21, 1704, carried on its title page, "Monsieur De Pourceaugnac or Squire Trelooby Acted at the Subscription Musick at the Theatre Royal in Lincoln's-Inn-Fields." In the preface to the second version, the anonymous author carefully points out, however, that his is not the acted version. He has included two scenes not present in the acted play, but otherwise, he suggests, his version has the same scenes and is of the same length as that acted; hence "I think I have justify'd the Title Page . . . ." We can conclude, however, that the title page notation, "Acted at . . . Lincoln's-Inn-Fields," was intended to sell copies and that the preface to the new or second edition is a rather lame attempt to explain why a published translation is needed. W. C. Ward, however, who produced the first scholarly edition of Vanbrugh, agreed with Sir Edmund Gosse that the second translation might, indeed, be the same as the Kit-Cat version.[56] At the same time, he noted that a slightly altered, third version of *Squire Trelooby* was printed in 1734 by James Ralph and was attributed to Vanbrugh and his two friends.

The answer to the puzzle about these three versions has not been forthcoming in spite of the best efforts of later scholars. Congreve's editor, Montague Summers, included the 1704, or second, *Squire Trelooby* in the Congreve canon as substantially the work of the collaborators; but Summers charges the three authors with "deliberate mystification."[57] Four years later John C. Hodges demonstrated that the anonymous second version was in fact by the industrious translator John Ozell and that Ozell had included the play in his own 1714 *The Works of Monsieur de Molière* (six volumes).[58] If Ozell is not a plagiary and if James Ralph is truthful in attributing the 1734 version (the third one) to a playhouse copy by Vanbrugh and his friends, then we must conclude that, in Vanbrugh's last revival on stage of *Squire Trelooby* in January 1706 he relied on the second version presumably because his own, the third one, was lost.

Nothing substantial has been added to our knowledge of the true Vanbrugh-Congreve-Walsh first play, but two recent articles have renewed the controversy. John Shipley concludes that the James Ralph version (number three) "represents basically the Walsh-Congreve-Vanbrugh adaptation first acted at Lincoln's Inn Fields on March 30, 1704"; but he wisely notes that the true state of affairs will be revealed only if the original Vanbrugh manuscript is someday uncovered. Graham D. Harley produces conclusive evidence, on the other hand, that James Ralph had plagiarized his version from Ozell's *Squire Trelooby* and that neither printed play represents the Walsh-Congreve-Vanbrugh collaboration.[59]

The premiere of *Squire Trelooby* in March 1704 featured "Select COMEDIANS from both Houses," with Doggett as Trelooby; Mrs. Bracegirdle as his daughter; Betterton as Lovewell; Cibber as Wimble; Penkethman as the Physician. It was the second least successful of Vanbrugh's contributions, with only eight performances in his lifetime, six more than *The Cuckold in Conceit*.

During the spring and summer of 1704, while the new playhouse in the Haymarket was being built, two events occurred that relate more to Vanbrugh's career as an architect than as a man of the theater but that show how rapidly he was becoming famous. On March 29, over the strenuous objections of the other heralds, he was appointed to the valuable post of Clarenceux King at Arms by Carlisle as his reward for building Castle Howard. This appointment was an honor that he was to treasure for the rest of his life. An even more momentous event that affected Vanbrugh indirectly was the Duke of Marlborough's victory over the French and the Bavarians at Blenheim on August 13; for, in less than five months, Marlborough was consulting with Vanbrugh about the construction of his magnificent country house in Woodstock Park, an enterprise that proved to be one of the poet's greatest achievements as well as a lifelong frustration.

VII   *Disaster at Queen's*

With the arrival of spring in 1705, Vanbrugh had assumed responsibilities that would have challenged all the best talents of two men. Blenheim was under construction, and the entire operation of the Haymarket Theatre was now in his hands. According to the *Diverting Post* of October 28, 1704, the playhouse had been nearly finished by that date. About the same time, Vanbrugh and Congreve, who had jointly directed the subscription drive for three thousand pounds to build the Queen's Theatre, were laying plans to assume the management of the new playhouse; and, by December 10, their efforts had come to the attention of the Society for the Reformation of Manners, Vanbrugh's old nemesis. On that date the society addressed a letter of protest to Archbishop Tenison that described Vanbrugh as "a man who had debauch'd the stage beyond the looseness of all former times" and that called for an immediate halt to the playwrights' scheme.[60] Nothing came of the objection, however, and within four days Vanbrugh and Congreve received Queen Anne's approval.

The language of the license must have appeared highly ironic to the Society for the Reformation of Manners for it began: "Whereas We have thought fitt for the better reforming the Abuses, and Imoralty [*sic*] of the Stage That a New Company of Comedians should be Establish'd for our Service, under Stricter Goverm^t and Regulations than have been formerly We therefore reposing especiall trust, and confidence in Our Trusty and Welbeloved John Vanbrugh & Willm Congreve Esq^{rs} . . . do Give and Grant unto them . . . full power & Authority to form, constitute, and Establish for Us, a Company of Comedians . . . ."[61] With the Queen's blessing on their enterprise, Vanbrugh and Congreve completed the necessary agreements with Betterton's company and bought its properties and costumes for nine hundred pounds;[62] and they then waited impatiently for the coming of spring when the first new London theater of the century would be properly prepared for use.

One of the curious facts of history is that a man so thoroughly English as Captain John Vanbrugh, whose massive structures persistently resisted Continental influence and whose plays fairly

radiated the spirit of John Bull's England, should have been responsible for the successful introduction of Italian opera into Great Bri-
tain. Its subsequent establishment there and in the United States in
later years, however, would never have occurred as it did had not
Vanbrugh, first, built the Queen's Theatre and, second, recognized
as its manager that only opera could flourish within its vast walls.
But the recognition came gradually, and only after a good many false
starts.

In casting about for a suitable play with which to open the new
theater in spring, Vanbrugh and Congreve decided upon an opera.
They probably would not have done so were it not for the success
the previous winter of Christopher Rich's Drury Lane production of
the opera *Arsinoe, Queen of Cyprus*, the work of Peter Motteux,
Thomas Clayton, Nicolino Haym, and Charles Dieupart.[63] Although the Rich production was advertised as performed "After the
Italian manner," it was sung by English singers in their own language. Following its premiere on January 16, 1705, *Arsinoe* was
performed nearly once each week throughout the rest of the season
and, on February 6, was offered at St. James's Palace as a birthday
present to Queen Anne. Congreve was asked to prepare the prologue for the royal occasion; but since he had already come to see
opera as a threat to the legitimate stage, he produced instead a
melancholy warning of the demise of the comic muse:

> No more shall she toil upon the Stage,
> And fruitless War with Vice and Folly Wage;
> No more in mean disguise she shall appear,
> And Shapes she wou'd reform be forced to wear;
> While Ignorance and Malice join to blame,
> And break the Mirror that reflects their Shame.[64]

Despite Congreve's reservations, Vanbrugh managed to persuade
his partner of the necessity of opening Queen's with an operatic
flourish; he even prevailed upon Congreve to provide the epilogue
by apparently convincing him that the new theater's main fare
would continue to be comedy.

The new playhouse was opened on April 9, 1705, with Giacome
Greber's pastoral opera *The Loves of Ergasto*, sung in Italian not by
Betterton's company but by a company from Italy ("the worst that
e're came from thence" according to John Downes, Betterton's
prompter).[65] From the Queen's Theatre receipts, Professor Avery

has been able to estimate the total seating of the playhouse capacity at more than seven hundred,[66] and Colley Cibber testifies to its vaulted spaciousness. From the very beginning, it was clear that the sheer size of Vanbrugh's theater would pose an almost insurmountable obstacle to its success. Cibber's description, for all its display of antagonism born of the rivalry between his company and Betterton's, gives us an accurate picture of the acoustical difficulties of the new house:

For what could their vast Columns, their guilded Cornices, their immoderate high Roofs avail, when scarce one Word in ten, could be distinctly heard in it? Nor had it, then, the Form, it now stands in [in 1740], which Necessity, two or three Years after reduc'd it to: At the first opening it, the flat Cieling, that is now over the Orchestre, was then a Semi-oval Arch, that sprung fifteen Feet higher from above the Cornice: The Cieling over the Pit too, was still more rais'd, being one level Line from the highest back part of the upper Gallery, to the Front of the Stage: The Front-boxes were a continued Semicircle, to the bare Walls of the House on each Side: This extraordinary, and superfluous Space occasion'd such an Undulation, from the Voice of every Actor, that generally what they said sounded like the Gabbling of so many People, in the lofty Isles in a Cathedral—[67]

To compound the problems offered by poor acoustics, Queen's was located in suburban London, well to the southwest of Drury Lane and Lincoln's Inn Fields and northwest of Westminster and Whitehall, where (Cibber added) there was nothing but pasture land, "from whence they could draw little, or no Sustenance, unless it were that of a Milk-Diet."

The epilogue that Congreve provided for the opening promised a return to legitimate theater after *The Loves of Ergasto* had run its course:

> Whatever future fate our house may find,
> At present we expect you shou'd be kind:
> Inconstancy itself can claim no right,
> Before enjoyment and the wedding night.
> You must be fix'd a little ere you range,
> You must be true till you have time to change.
> But we pretend not to a honeymoon.
>   . . .
> To sound and shew at first we make pretence,
> In time we may regale you with some sense,
> But that at present were too great expence.
>   . . .

The day's at hand when we shall shift the scene,
And to yourselves shew your dear selves again.
Paint the reverse of what you've seen to-day,
And in bold strokes the vicious town display.[68]

After a five day run, *The Loves of Ergasto* appeared only twice more
and then as a shortened three part musical afterpiece to the
anonymous play *The Consultation*. A string of failures followed the
opera, although, as Congreve had promised, Betterton's company
revived a number of their past successes; but the old ware was not
popular and Queen's closed on June 29, 1705. It remained dark for
four months, while fifteen hundred men labored under Vanbrugh at
Blenheim and while Betterton returned to the old tennis court theater in Lincoln's Inn Fields. For the time being, the state of theatrical affairs in London was a mockery of Garth's optimistic pro-
nouncement in the prologue to *Ergasto:* "And stages thrive, as
churches did before."

Congreve withdrew from the managership shortly after this first
season ended, and Vanbrugh was now so deeply in debt that he was
never again to be entirely free of financial cares. The prologue he
supplied for *The Confederacy* at the opening of the Queen's the
following October laughed at the poverty of poets, but his situation
that fall was no joke; his Kit-Cat associate Arthur Mainwaring, the
intimate of the Duchess of Marlborough and the lover of Anne
Oldfield, wrote to the duchess in the summer of 1708: "I am sorry
for him, because I believe he is unhappy through his own folly, and
I can see no reasonable way to help. What I mean by his folly, is his
building the playhouse, which certainly cost him a great deal more
than was subscribed; and his troubles arise from the workmen that
built it, and the tradesmen that furnished the cloaths, &c, for the
actors."[69] In late 1719 Vanbrugh regarded the Haymarket venture
as the source of all his ill: "I have no money to dispose of. I have
been many years at hard Labour, to work thorough the Cruel
Difficultys, that HayMarket [*sic*] undertaking involv'd me in; notwithstanding the aid, of a large Subscription Nor are those difficultys, quite at an end yet" (IV, 123). The Queen's Theatre may have
risen from the ashes, as it were, of the Phoenix Inn; but since its
future was none too certain, its architect and manager was to bear
for life the burden of its failure.

The opening of the Queen's Theatre for the 1705–1706 season was necessarily delayed until Vanbrugh had completed the summer of building for the Duke of Marlborough. When the new playhouse began its first full season on October 30, the featured play was no other than one more translated comedy by Vanbrugh, *The Confederacy*. It is impossible to believe with Laurence Whistler that Vanbrugh had produced this best of his adaptations during the previous summer "holiday," especially when it was followed in December by *The Mistake*, still another of his adaptations.[70] Both plays must have been largely completed by him during the preceding winter and perhaps earlier.

The Confederacy was the translation of another of those French comedies that Vanbrugh may have seen in Paris (and his second borrowing from Dancourt), *Les Bourgeoises à la Mode* (1682). Thoroughly Englished, heavily marked with Vanbrugh's gift for comic detail and with his addition of touches of wit and satire, the new version was a lively performance. *The Confederacy* deserved its modest success; it ran for five consecutive performances and was revived another six times before the season ended.

Close upon the heels of *The Confederacy* came *The Mistake*, another effort to save the new playhouse from disaster. Once again Vanbrugh's command of French resulted in a close prose translation, this time of Molière's *Le Depit Amoureux* (1656). Although first announced for December 10, *The Mistake* had its premiere on December 27, 1705, with Betterton—"majestic in decay"—acting Don Alvarez. The play served its purpose in helping Queen's to survive, but it proved to be a failure during Vanbrugh's lifetime, with only eight more performances after January 1706.

Throughout the remainder of the 1705–1706 season, Vanbrugh felt keenly the competition with Drury Lane; for both companies were trying to reach the same audience with essentially the same kind of fare—a mixture of comedy and tragedy interspersed with opera. In rapid succession after *The Mistake*, Vanbrugh revived and presented *The Provok'd Wife* on January 19 and *Squire Trelooby* on January 28, "the last act being entirely new."[71] When comedies seemed unable to meet the competition, Vanbrugh turned to operas. He tried George Granville's *The British Enchanters* with some success, and he followed it with Pierre Motteux's *The Temple of Love* which had none. When *Camilla*, by Owen Swiney and

Niccolo Haym, was well received at Drury Lane in late March, Vanbrugh countered in April with Tom D'Urfey's fantastic *Wonders in the Sun, or The Kingdom of Birds*, a comic ballad opera that satirized Italian opera.[72] Although it was performed five times and although its songs were featured at the end of the season as entr'acte entertainment, *Wonders in the Sun* did not meet half the expenses incurred; and—like all of Vanbrugh's theatrical ventures—it failed to rescue the Queen's Theatre from its financial morass.

VIII *Toward Union*

The only answer to the curse on both the houses was a union—a return to the state of affairs before Betterton and his crew had bolted from Drury Lane. Vanbrugh had already petitioned the lord chamberlain to unite the companies, but Rich objected that his actors were happy as things were and that ruin would follow union.[73] Congreve, safely sidelined with lethargy and the gout, wrote his friend Joseph Keally in April that Queen's could not last another season. By now, Vanbrugh was once again too busy at building houses and with his duties as herald to be troubled by the demands of the playhouse; hence he turned the theater over to the company to make what they could during the summer. On August 14, 1706, he stopped managing the theater and rented it for seven years to Owen Swiney, Rich's associate, for the very low figure of five pounds per acting day up to a maximum of seven hundred pounds for the 1706–1707 season.[74]

For a time, it appeared that the two theaters in London would reach a satisfactory division of labor. Rich agreed to let Swiney add the best actors from Drury Lane to those at the Haymarket, while Rich would produce operas and spectacular entertainments at the smaller houses—Drury Lane and Dorset Gardens—with the remaining singers and dancers. According to Cibber, the apparent union of the actors was part of Rich's grand design to hold clandestine control of both playhouses. But, while Swiney succeeded in gaining better audiences than had Vanbrugh, the arrangement was an unlikely one, as a man of the theater like Congreve could readily see. Just before the season began, he wrote to Keally of the new state of affairs:

The playhouses have undergone another revolution; and Swinny, with Wilks, Mrs. Oldfield, Pinkethman, Bullock, and Dicky, are come over to the Hay-Market. Vanbrugh resigns his authority to Swinny, which occasioned the revolt. Mr. Rich complains and rails like Volpone when counterplotted by Mosca. My Lord Chamberlain approves and ratifies the desertion; and the design is, to have plays only at the Hay-Market; and operas only at Covent Garden. I think the design right to restore acting; but the houses are misapplied, which time may change.[75]

The time would come shortly when Vanbrugh would effect the change by firmly establishing opera at the Queen's Theatre and plays at Drury Lane.

For the next year, Vanbrugh was relatively free of management affairs except for minor skirmishes with Rich, who had resorted to the courts in order to punish Swiney and Vanbrugh for keeping the Drury Lane actors. Swiney flourished at the Haymarket, quickly clearing himself (according to Cibber) of his two hundred pound debt to Rich; and Vanbrugh must have looked with a hungry eye upon his recipe for success. It appears that Vanbrugh was instrumental in suggesting to Lord Halifax the three benefit plays that he underwrote in January, for Halifax was not only a patron of letters but also a fellow Kit-Cat in whose company Vanbrugh had gone the previous summer to invest Prince George of Hanover with the Order of the Garter. According to Cibber, Halifax was so zealous in his encouragement of the benefit productions that the subscription was quickly sold out.

Also in the entourage of Halifax in the preceding summer was Joseph Addison, whose English opera *Rosamond* opened on March 4, 1707, at Rich's Drury Lane opera house. Vanbrugh must also have been more than casually interested in that event, for the opera was not only a dramatic tribute to the Duke of Marlborough but it featured on stage an enormous model of Vanbrugh's Blenheim Palace. In the opera, Fair Rosamond, of ballad and chronicle fame, had been the mistress of King Henry II; and the manor so closely associated with her name was situated in Woodstock Park where Blenheim was rising. Besides praising Marlborough, Addison had intended to establish a native opera with a theme that was intelligible to Englishmen and in music that was more suited to their temperament. But subscriptions failed; the music was unsatisfactory; and, because the actor George Powell appeared on stage (to speak the prologue to the opera) against the lord chamberlain's orders, Rich's company was temporarily suspended from acting.[76]

Rosamond had two more performances in that month and was never
seen thereafter on stage.

With the end of the 1706–1707 season, Vanbrugh's playwriting
came to an end. It may be that he provided a final comedy for the
Queen's Theatre on March 22, 1707, with the acting of *The Cuckold
in Conceit*, a translation of Molière's *Sganarelle*, or *Le Cocu Imag-
inaire*. Cibber, at least, says so; but Cibber's memory is not always
reliable. No other reference to Vanbrugh's responsibility for the
farce is extant in the stage literature of the eighteenth century. The
likelihood that Vanbrugh had some hand in the Molière work is
strengthened slightly by the fact that it appeared as an afterpiece to
George Granville's *The British Enchanters*, the opera that he had
brought on stage at Queen's the year before. Granville was, of
course, a Kit-Cat; and the production of *The British Enchanters*
featured "the intire front prospect of Blenheim Castle." *The Cuckold in Conceit* was advertised on May 24, 1709, in the *Daily Courant*
for a second and final performance on June 1; but it seems on that
date to have been replaced by Farquhar's *The Stratagem* for William
Bowen's benefit.

On May 7, 1707, Vanbrugh extended Swiney's lease to fourteen
years and turned his full attention to architecture. Throughout the
building season of 1707, he continued his supervision of the work at
Castle Howard and Blenheim; and he laid plans for remodelling
Kimbolton Castle for the Earl of Manchester. In the meantime, Sir
Thomas Skipwith, Rich's "silent" partner, decided abruptly to shed
his share in the Drury Lane patent and the troubles that went with
it. According to Cibber's account in the *Apology*, Skipwith gave his
interest for a token amount to Colonel Henry Brett, claiming that he
had made nothing from it for the past ten years but was certain that
Brett could do better.[77] Brett promptly proceeded, upon the advice
of his old friend Cibber, to gain joint possession of all Drury Lane
property and to make plans to bring back the actors who had fled to
the Queen's Theatre in the Haymarket.

IX *The First Opera Impresario*

Colonel Brett and Rich began the new season at Drury Lane with
a run of comedies, and Swiney at Queen's did the same; something
had to be done to avert financial disaster. Once again Vanbrugh
decided to try to bring about a union of the actors that would place
them at Drury Lane to act plays and would leave the Queen's

Theatre to present operas. This time, however, he had allies; for Brett was already of the same mind and could prevent Rich from interference because of his close friendship with the Marquis of Kent, then lord chamberlain. Vanbrugh, of course, could bring to bear the heaviest artillery, for he had influence with the queen herself through the Duke of Marlborough. On December 31, 1707, the lord chamberlain issued a royal order that after January 10, 1708, Drury Lane would be the royal playhouse and Queen's would be the royal opera house. [78]

Now that Vanbrugh's plan had succeeded, he attempted to re-coup his lost thousands: he bought Owen Swiney's interest, retained him only as manager, and set to work to make opera thrive. Until now, the only clear evidence of the date of Vanbrugh's repurchase appears in his letter to Manchester of February 24, 1708; but a letter from singer Anna Lodi (to Swiney?) regarding the performance of Christopher Pepusch's *Thomyris* and dated January 10, 1708, estab-lishes the fact that Vanbrugh was signing contracts with the perform-ers on the effective date of the lord chamberlain's order. [79] And I am now able to date a previously undated letter to Vice-Chamberlain Thomas Coke that confirms Vanbrugh's return by January 20, 1708, to an active interest in Queen's; for this epistle indicates how deeply Vanbrugh was involved in negotiations for singers, how high his expectations for income were, and how influential he was in stopping competition. [80]

Despite Vanbrugh's best efforts throughout the winter and spring, the receipts at Queen's continued to remain far below his expectations. A manuscript account that Vanbrugh submitted on April 7, 1708, makes all too plain the extent of his financial losses at the season's end. [81] From his figures, the daily cost of an opera was £ 116.; the total expenses for twenty-three performances from January 13 through April 6 were £ 4,090.; and the loss was £ 1,146. Then comes the obvious conclusion: "By this Account it appears. That Altho' the Queen shou'd be pleas'd to Allow a Thousand pounds a Year towards Salarys; And that the Towne shou'd by Sub-scriptions take off the Load of Cloaths & Scenes; the Daily Charge wou'd Still rise to full a hundred pounds a day; Which is the most the House can ever hope to receive the Season throughout One Performance with an Other——[Endorsed 'Mr Vanbrugg State of ye Opera Account']." [82]

These figures shed much light on Vanbrugh's bitter complaint of

May 14 when he wrote Vice-Chamberlain Thomas Coke regarding a final accounting for the season.[83] After characterizing himself as "so Vast a Sufferer by this Years Adventure," he defended his appearance of niggardliness: "I must upon the whole, beg you to believe, That on any of these occasions 'tis my nature & my principle to overdo, rather than have the least pretence for Complaint. But I am so hard run in this unhappy Business, that there is no room left for Generosity: If I can at last comply wth what in rigour I ought, 'tis the utmost I can hope for. I therefore beg you will have a favourable opinion of my Intentions in all these Struggles. And if in any particular I come Something short of what you think should be; lay it to my want of Power to do better. . . ."

It was a sad thing, indeed, for a man who had begun his career in the theater with generous gifts to the actors of his third night money to be reduced to this extremity, even more so when he was currently employed as architect to England's most glorious military hero since the Middle Ages. By May 11, 1708, when he wrote to the Earl of Manchester, he had sold the company to Swiney for the second and last time. Henceforth, his only concern about Queen's Theatre, Haymarket, was to collect the rent.

Vanbrugh's contribution to the establishment and growth of opera in England can hardly be exaggerated. During the winter and spring of 1708, his letters to Manchester indicate his desire to bring to England the most competent Italian singers; and his efforts were most dramatically rewarded with the arrival of contralto Nicolino Grimaldi, or Signor Nicolini, in the late fall. Nicolini made his debut in the remodelled Queen's theater on December 14, 1708, in Niccolo Haym's *Pyrrhus and Demetrius* and was an instantaneous success. "Thus began," says John Palmer, with a thumb of his nose at Italian opera, "the importation of foreign singers, whose evil result is, after two hundred years, not yet extinguished."[84] Vanbrugh introduced, as well, the pattern of twice weekly performances, thus permitting the company to make the elaborate costume and staging preparations needed for each opera. And, most significant, he was responsible for establishing opera in the Haymarket and plays at Drury Lane. From a meteoric beginning as a comic dramatist, Vanbrugh had become in a dozen years England's most influential operatic impresario, an achievement that some of his countrymen were reluctant to acknowledge as a forward step for the stage.[85]

Although Vanbrugh could see clearly the faults in his management that had led to the failure of the opera—beginning late in the season, extravagant expenditures, lack of support by patrons who thought the enterprise already a financial success, and his inability to look after all affairs personally—he was nevertheless certain that opera would thrive in London.[86] In 1710–1711, the watershed season, Swiney, Robert Wilks, Cibber, and Doggett established a system of management at Drury Lane that proved stable for twenty years; and the production at the Queen's Theatre of Handel's *Rinaldo*—with Nicolini in the title role—finally established the popularity of opera. For the 1712–1713 season John James Heidegger succeeded Swiney as lessee and retained his connection with Queen's until 1749.

Vanbrugh's interest in both playhouses continued for many years beyond his last season of opera management in 1708: in 1713 and 1714 he was forced to appeal to the lord chamberlain because the Drury Lane managers had failed to pay the agreed upon rent for costumes and properties taken from the Haymarket theater. On October 13, 1720, Sir John assigned his share in Queen's (now King's) to his brother Charles,[87] but he continued to maintain his interest in opera as one of the directors of the Royal Academy of Music, headed by his good friend Newcastle and established to encourage operatic performances in general and Handel's music in particular. Vanbrugh's letters to Tonson and Carlisle in the 1720's also show his concern that opera succeed, although in one he deplores the fact that "with all this encouragement from the Towne, not a fresh Poet Appears; they are forc'd to Act round and round upon the Old Stock, though Cibber tells me, 'tis not to be conceiv'd, how many and how bad Plays, are brought to them."[88] Earlier in that same year (April 6, 1722), he had written to Lord Carlisle, "Musick has taken deep root with us" (IV, 141). It was an accomplishment for which he deserved much of the credit.

Two coincidences in Vanbrugh's theatrical career are intriguing, for a calendar of his comedies shows that once every ten years during his lifetime there was an unusually large number of performances. Not counting the 1696–1697 season and the triumphal production in succession of three Vanbrugh plays, the pattern began in earnest in the 1705–1706 season with thirty-seven performances of his plays, continued in 1715–1716 with thirty-one performances,

and concluded in 1725-1726 with a remarkable thirty-nine performances. Vanbrugh's death in March 1726 was followed, appropriately enough, by a succession of his plays on stage: all eight of his
acknowledged comedies (excluding *Squire Trelooby* and *The Cuckold in Conceit*) played at least once at Drury Lane or at Lincoln's Inn
Fields in the first three months of the 1726-1727 season.

The second coincidence is that Vanbrugh's very last stage
success—like his very first—intertwined his name as a dramatic
poet with that of Colley Cibber. Captain Vanbrugh had begun his
playwriting career in 1696 when he wrote a successful sequel to
Cibber's *Love's Last Shift;* his career ended posthumously with
Cibber's revision for the stage of Vanbrugh's uncompleted *A Journey to London.* When *The Provok'd Husband* opened at Drury Lane
on January 10, 1728, the audience at first wrongly attributed the low
material to the unpopular Cibber and hissed throughout at the
Wronghead scenes. Mrs. Anne Oldfield, however, who played Lady
Townly, received one misdirected hiss as she began the Epilogue.
According to Thomas Davies, she fixed her eye immediately upon
the author of the hiss, "made a very short pause, and spoke the
words *poor creature!* loud enough to be heard by the audience, with
such a look of mingled scorn, pity, and contempt, that the most
uncommon applause justified her conduct in this particular. . . ."[89]
Cibber stepped forward at the end of the play to explain that Vanbrugh had in fact written the condemned parts and that the audience's prejudice toward himself had led to the misdirected his-
sing.[90]

The Cibber-Vanbrugh collaboration survived its tumultuous
premiere; it went on stage for twenty-eight consecutive nights until
driven from the scene by *The Beggar's Opera.* It brought in more
money, said Cibber, than any other play at Drury Lane in the
preceding fifty years. What's more, it had greater success than any
of Cibber's six comedies; and, by the end of the century, *The Provok'd Husband* (staged 434 times) had outperformed by a wide mar-
gin Vanbrugh's two other original plays, *The Relapse* (238) and *The
Provok'd Wife* (342).

CHAPTER 3

The Relapse

I *The Making of a Sequel*

IN January 1696, when Captain Vanbrugh saw the comedy *Love's Last Shift: or, The Fool in Fashion* performed at the Theatre Royal in Drury Lane, a single literary event dramatically began his career. At thirty-two, Vanbrugh was at the height of his intellectual powers; he was older by nine years than William Congreve at his first play; older than most of the other successful comic playwrights at the start of their dramatic careers; and older, above all, than the pert upstart Colley Cibber who had written *The Fool in Fashion.* Moreover, the ending of Cibber's comedy, with its reformed rake, invited a sequel; for no episode of *The Perils of Pauline* could have left the audience more eager for the next installment. Vanbrugh began to write, and he submitted in early April to the patentees a finished comedy, "Got, Conceived, and Born," as he claimed in the Prologue, "in six weeks space" (I, 13).[1]

The success of Colley Cibber's new comedy had been in large measure due to the actor's stage interpretation of Sir Novelty Fashion. Charles Sackville, Earl of Dorset, told Cibber "That it was the best, First Play, that any Author in his Memory, had produc'd; and that for a young Fellow, to shew himself such an Actor, and such a Writer, in one Day, was something extraordinary."[2] Captain Vanbrugh, too, was impressed by Cibber's interpretation; he was so much impressed that, when his sequel, *The Relapse*, was to be staged, he preferred the young actor Cibber for the role in his play of Baron Foppington.

But Cibber's play itself, more than the stage interpretation, inspired Vanbrugh to write a continuation of *Love's Last Shift.* It is frequently asserted, of course, that Vanbrugh intended *The Relapse* to correct the poor psychology of Cibber's play. Bonamy Dobrée, to whom we are indebted for one of the most scholarly editions of any

63

Restoration comic playwright, believes that the fifth act reformation
of Loveless in *Love's Last Shift* struck Vanbrugh as "absurdly contrary to likelihood, certainly at variance with his own observation of
men and women."[3] Paul Mueschke and Jeannette Fleisher in "A
Re-evaluation of Vanbrugh" draw the conclusion that "Vanbrugh's
general attitude was certainly antagonistic to this absurd portrayal of
the reformative power of virtue in reclaiming a confirmed rake, and
The Relapse was his answer to it." The latest biographer of Colley
Cibber concurs, and three recent doctoral dissertations on Vanbrugh arrive at essentially the same conclusion.[4]

It is by no means inevitable, however, that Cibber's audience or
any audience must regard the ending of *Love's Last Shift* as
psychologically invalid. It is illogical, of course, for a stage rake or
any rake to effect a permanent reformation. But logic in this case has
little to do with psychology, for such reformations do occur in life.
More often than not, perhaps, the penitent sinner, sincere for the
moment in his protestations of future fidelity, seizes a convenient
opportunity to fall again. Vanbrugh knew that, but so did Cibber. As
we can see in a brief resumé of the story line of *Love's Last Shift*,
Cibber not only prepared for Loveless's transformation with considerable care for its psychological verisimilitude but also hinted that it
might not be permanent.

Love's Last Shift opens with Loveless's servant Snap berating his
master for drunkenness and prodigality. In the first year of his marriage, we learn, Loveless grew weary of his beautiful wife; in the
second year he whored, drank, gamed, ran into debt, and left England to escape his creditors. From the third through the seventh
year, he toured Europe in style; and in the eighth through the tenth
year, he grew poor. Now penniless, and sure that his wife is dead,
he hopes to redeem his mortgaged property; but his former friend
Young Worthy protects the still-living Amanda from Loveless's pre-
dations with a scheme to reunite the couple. Young Worthy, of
course, has a second "shift" in mind—to gain the five thousand
pound fortune of Narcissa, daughter of Sir William Wisewoud,
whom Sir William intends to be the bride of Worthy's elder brother.

A key to Loveless's fifth act redemption comes in the next scene:
Amanda, we discover, has just inherited two thousand pounds a
year from her only relation. Loveless hardly needs a stronger motive
for reforming. We learn as well that Amanda has been true to virtue
in spite of her husband's neglect. After announcing to Amanda that

her husband has returned from Europe, refined in lewdness, Young Worthy argues that Loveless has only been fashionably vicious and that, if Amanda can by some artifice "pass upon him as a new mistress," Loveless might be won back by seeing that his wife still possesses sexual appeal. Amanda agrees, at length, to the plan.

Act II is largely a display of the stage qualities of Cibber's egregious coxcomb, Sir Novelty Fashion, who believes himself the style-setter for London. He professes himself to be as well a ladies' man; and, when Narcissa asks why he loves her, he replies: "'Tis a Province I never undertake, I must confess; I think 'tis sufficient, if I tell a Lady why she shou'd love me."[5] Young Worthy and Narcissa, meanwhile, are on the verge of reaching an agreement to marry as the act ends. In Act III, after her friend Hillaria encourages Amanda to carry out Worthy's shift without fear that Loveless will discover the deception, we are entertained again by Sir Novelty, who proposes marriage to Narcissa and is turned down by Sir William Wisewoud because, as Sir William says, "You take such an extravagant Care in the clothing of your Body, that your Understanding goes naked for't."[6] At St. James's Park later, Amanda catches her first glimpse of Loveless in "pinching poverty" but still pursuing whores; and she returns home to await his coming.

In Act IV, Sir Novelty flirts with his mistress, Mrs. Flareit; for he thinks she is Narcissa. Thus Cibber introduces two last shifts of love: in one, a lady pretends to be a whore; in the other, a whore, to be a lady. Arrived at Amanda's house, Loveless is surprised at the elegant lodgings. When Amanda enters and they embrace, she cries out that he is the wrong man. Loveless, thinking he has stumbled on an intrigue, tries to turn it to his own advantage by courting her since he finds he desires her. Amanda declares pleasure to be the end of life, and they retire. In the final act, Amanda delivers her apostrophe to virtue, mystifies Loveless with allusions to her fidelity, and reveals herself with a tattoo for proof as his wife. Loveless, roused from his deep "Lethargy of Vice," kneels at her feet and vows to "wash [his] Crimes in never-ceasing Tears of Penitence."[7] In the final scene, we glimpse Sir Novelty Fashion once again, and the Young Worthy–Narcissa subplot is brought to a happy end. The play concludes with a brief masque and with Loveless's protestations that, while he is with Amanda, the world must see the happiness of marriage and "the Folly of a wandring Passion."

In two places in *Love's Last Shift*, as we can see, Cibber was careful to hint that Loveless's reformation is a temporary one, that it results from his poverty and Amanda's sex appeal—not from a change of heart. In the final scene, the song of Reason in the masque warns that the delights of love are transitory: "Cease, cease, fond Fools, your empty Noise,/ And follow not such idle Joys:/ Love gives you but a short-liv'd Bliss,/ But I bestow immortal Happiness."[8] The character Marriage agrees that happiness in love is only temporary and that a wife is a "galling Yoke." And Loveless, in that same concluding scene, inadvertently points to a future fall when he says that his happiness will last *while he is in Amanda's arms.*

Furthermore, Cibber emphasizes throughout the comedy Loveless's virtual dedication to depravity. From his first appearance on stage—when he explains to Young Worthy that he has returned because he considers London to be "a place of uninterrupted Pleasure"[9]—to the scene at St. James's park, and to that in Amanda's house, when he says of the maidservant, "If her Lady don't make a little haste, I find I shall present my humble Service to her,"[10] Loveless is depicted as whole-heartedly devoted to sexual pleasures. He is not likely, in short, to change permanently his libertine nature.

At the same time, Cibber took care to make Loveless's apparent reformation a believable one. His redemption from vice, we must recall, comes after nearly ten years of debauchery and at a time when he is penniless and nearly friendless. Snap's description of his own situation applies equally to Loveless's: "I thank Heav'n, that I have so much Grace left, that I can repent, when I have no more Opportunities of being wicked."[11] For an attractive and wealthy wife (who has remained true) to win back such a man for a time seems not so improbable as we are supposed to believe. Furthermore, a man like Loveless, who has passed his thirtieth year, is not likely to be consumed by passions as powerful as those of his youth; moreover, his remaining passion could have been satisfied by the lovely Amanda, "charming beyond the Wishes of luxurious Love."[12] Had that passion been mixed with reason, it might have been enough to prove wrong the old tenet of courtly love that insisted that one could find ecstasy only outside of marriage. Moreover, Amanda insists that she can change and thus remain endlessly desirable, and we recall that Millamant's provisos in Congreve's *The Way of the World* were designed to ensure that she would be courted the same way after marriage as before it so that she and Mirabell would find the endless variety that all lovers seek.

Nevertheless, in uniting Loveless and Amanda after nearly ten years of separation, Cibber made no promises that Loveless would remain faithful. Surely we cannot believe, as Amanda did when Loveless first courted her, that it is "impossible for a Man to forswear himself when he made Love" (Loveless's words, Act V, scene 2). We, like Captain John Vanbrugh, would expect Cibber's hero to fall again at the first opportunity of "being wicked," but to do so with caution and not so frequently, in order to preserve the financial security and the comfortable life that his reunion with Amanda had brought him.[13]

Vanbrugh, as a matter of fact, had thought Loveless's reformation convincing; but he quickly found himself speculating about the changes that time might bring. In "A Short Vindication of *The Relapse* and *The Provok'd Wife*," he described his reaction to Cibber's play as follows:

> I observ'd in a Play, called *Love's Last Shift, or the Fool in Fashion*, a Debauchee pay so dear for his Lewdness, and his Folly, as from a plentiful Fortune, and a Creditable Establishment in the World, to be reduc'd by his Extravagance to want even the Common Supports of Life.
>
> In this Distress, Providence . . . by an unexpected turn in his favour, restores him to Peace and Plenty: And there is that in the manner of doing it, and the Instrument that brings it to pass, as must necessarily give him the most sensible View, both of his Misery past, from the Looseness of his life; and his Happiness to come in the Reform of it. In the close of the Play, he's left thoroughly convinc'd it must therefore be done, and as fully determin'd to do it.
>
> For my part, *I thought him so undisputably in the right;* and he appear'd to me to be got into so agreeable a Tract of Life, that I often took pleasure to indulge a musing Fancy, and suppose myself in his place.[14]

Vanbrugh, we see, was not so unacquainted with the world that he did not understand that such reformations could occur, but the "pleasure" that he indulges is to imagine what will happen to Loveless when his present love begins to cloy and when temptation is once again thrown in his way. It was not, therefore, any dispute of Cibber's understanding of the psychology of the rake that made Vanbrugh write; it was rather that he saw the possibilities of a new

play on the same subject—one with a suggestive title that was
bound to help it to succeed.

The bed trick device that had so impressed Vanbrugh was not
original with Cibber, of course; indeed, De Witt C. Croissant
suggests that it is at least remotely related to Shakespeare's *All's
Well that Ends Well* and to James Shirley's *Gamester*;[15] and it
certainly has something in common with Shakespeare's *Measure for Measure* and the trick by which Angelo is brought to bed
with his own betrothed Mariana. Nor is the reclamation of the straying spouse new: Mr. B. R. S. Fone offers several earlier dramas in
which such a reformation takes place and reminds us that Cibber
refers in the Epilogue to Loveless's transformation as such "out of
fashion stuff!"[16] What was original, however, was Cibber's mixture
in *Love's Last Shift* not only of the comedy of manners that Sir
George Etherege, William Wycherley, and Congreve had so brilliantly defined but also of the sentimentalism of such lesser writers
as Thomas Shadwell, Tom D'Urfey, and Aphra Behn.[17] And this
mixture was to influence the plays of George Farquhar, Sir Richard
Steele, Susanna Centlivre, and—of course—Cibber's nearest im-
itator, Sir John Vanbrugh. It was, as well, the predecessor of
(though not necessarily an influence upon) the wit tempered with
morality that characterized the *Tatler* and *Spectator*, some of
Samuel Richardson, Thomas Gray, and a host of third rate
eighteenth century playwrights.

What Cibber began and Vanbrugh continued—both of them by
accident rather than design, for the reform of English comedy was
the last thing they contemplated—was a new emphasis upon emo-
tion rather than upon wit in the relationships among characters. As
Leonard Ashley so effectively states, in Cibber's comedy,

the stock characters of the Restoration comedy of manners were purged of
their vices (but retained, fortunately, some of their old spirit and dash) and
presented to the audience as models of virtue to be emulated rather than as
horrible examples of what to avoid. Instead of starting, like Jonson, with
"manners," creating caricatures to embody "humors" and a plot to exhibit
and satirize them, Cibber—rather like the writer of the nineteenth-century
thesis play—starts with a moral problem. His play is devoted to stating it
and resolving it. He brings his essentially good people—even his wayward
protagonist is an "honest" rake—from distress to happiness.[18]

So successful had Cibber been and so far had sentimentalism taken
over by 1721 that in that year Cibber bowdlerized his own play: he

softened the language to eliminate such words as "naked in bed," "stinking breath," and "maidenhead"; and he also omitted the first scene of Act IV, an oathy altercation between Sir William Wisewoud and two bullies.[19]

Although a moral main plot is Cibber's chief contribution to English sentimental comedy, his Sir Novelty Fashion ranks as a classic figure of foppish fun; for this character held the stage throughout much of the next century as the exemplar of snuff-dipping affectation and of self-adulating coxcombry. Cibber the actor was to have no major role after Sir Novelty until he took the stage the following season as Lord Foppington in Vanbrugh's *The Relapse*; but, when he did, the old Sir Novelty had been further refined. He was less rude and vulgar, and he had fewer opportunities for farcical action. It is difficult to say, in either play, which is the central character—the reformed rake or the affected fop.

II *The Plot of* The Relapse

The play that Vanbrugh provided as a sequel relied heavily upon *The Fool in Fashion* for its situation and main characters. But, unlike Cibber's well-made comedy, Vanbrugh's play ignored the unity of action most flagrantly, dividing itself into two distinct parts that vied with each other for center stage. The two part construction, a feature that gave Jeremy Collier the chance to choose his own main plot for attack, can be seen clearly in a brief synopsis. In Act I, Loveless, in his opening soliloquy, reveals his contentment in a retired life with Amanda; but, as they talk about his impending trip to London, she expresses dismay at his determination to make the journey a proof of his new-found virtue. In Scene 2, which introduces the subplot, young Tom Fashion, who is the brother of Lord Foppington and who has just returned penniless from Italy, decides to apply to his elder brother for money. When Lord Foppington ignores Tom, the younger brother is ready to listen to the scheme of Coupler, the matchmaker who has arranged a marriage between his older brother and a wealthy country girl. Tom, however, determines to give his brother one more chance before he will embrace Coupler's plot to substitute Tom for Foppington.

In Act II, the major plot continues with Loveless and Amanda ensconced in London lodgings. No sooner has he finished telling Amanda of a handsome woman he admired at the playhouse than by coincidence the very woman appears—Berinthia, Amanda's widowed cousin. When Lord Foppington soon arrives to pay his compliments to his old acquaintance, he manages instead to flirt with Amanda and to fence with Loveless. His departure with a slight wound is balanced by the entrance of the elder Worthy, who has also taken a liking to Amanda, and who—when the two men leave—is proposed by Berinthia as a suitable instrument for Amanda's revenge should Loveless ever betray her. In Act III, after an opening scene in which Lord Foppington turns Tom away and the younger brother vows revenge, the serious action proceeds to further complications: Loveless and Berinthia discover they are in love. Worthy, formerly Berinthia's lover, has observed all and now proposes a plan: Berinthia will help to make Amanda jealous of Loveless's supposed mistress; Worthy will then propose himself to Amanda as a means of revenge; Berenthia and Loveless will be free to conduct their amours; and, after a "short campaign," Worthy and Berinthia can return to their old relationship. As the scene ends, Berinthia begins to encourage Amanda's doubts about her husband's faithfulness.

A major shift of scene now occurs with the arrival of Young Fashion and his servant Lory at the country house of Sir Tunbelly Clumsey, the well-to-do father of Lord Foppington's betrothed, Hoyden, where Tom quickly convinces Tunbelly that he is Lord Foppington. In the meantime, in Scene 4, Hoyden receives with delight the news of the arrival of her fiancé; and she rushes, her Nurse behind her, to put on her best smock. In another room, Tom is dismayed to learn that he must wait a week for fulfillment of his plan, and his suggestion that a prompt wedding will save money only reinforces Tunbelly's resolution to make it a proper affair.

In Act IV, Miss Hoyden, whose desire for a husband is exceeded only by her passion for city life, is easily persuaded by Tom to marry him the next day; and the two of them enlist the help of Nurse, who is to offer Chaplain Bull a church benefice—and her own hand in marriage—if he will perform the ceremony. In Scene 2, the action shifts again to Loveless's lodgings, where Berinthia pursues her design to recommend Worthy as a gallant for Amanda. Although the hour is late, Worthy arrives to report that Loveless will not be home until three or four o'clock; and Berinthia proposes a card game for their amusement. Not long after, Loveless enters Berinthia's apartment in the dark, waits for her return, and carries her—crying for help *very softly*—into the bedroom.

Meanwhile, back at Tunbelly's in Scene 4, Hoyden and Tom have been married. But, when word comes that Lord Foppington has arrived, Tom has to act quickly to convince the family that the new arrival is an imposter. When Sir Tunbelly meets the real Lord Foppington at the gate, he drives away his footmen in Scene 5; and he then proceeds in Scene 6 to disarm the peer and bind him. Hoyden suggests that he be dragged through the horse pond, and Tom turns down Foppington's offer of five thousand pounds if he will reveal the jest. But a neighbor, Sir John Friendly, arrives opportunely, identifies the true Lord Foppington, and Tom flees. Sir Tunbelly Clumsey is only momentarily discomfitted, and Hoyden is not discomfitted at all, for she is as ready to marry the second lord as she was to wed the first.

In Act V, Tom Fashion, in London again, learns from Coupler of Hoyden's marriage to Lord Foppington; but he also learns that the entire retinue will soon be in town where it will perhaps be possible to influence Nurse and Bull to reveal the earlier marriage. In Scene 2, after Worthy appeals for Berinthia's continued assistance in his effort to seduce Amanda, Berinthia promises to give Amanda a glimpse of Loveless's mistress and thereby make Amanda more pliable to Worthy's solicitations. Alone with Amanda, Berinthia discourses wittily about man's fickleness and arranges to show evidence of it in Loveless. In another part of London, at Young Fashion's lodgings, Tom convinces Nurse that he will be a good husband to Hoyden; and he and Coupler promise the Chaplain the living of Fat-Goose parish when Tom and Hoyden's marriage is properly recognized.

The next scene (4) brings the serious action to its climax and partial resolution. Amanda has now seen the proof Berinthia promised and contemplates taking revenge. But, when Worthy offers her his love, Amanda responds that she cannot think about love again and that their revenge would be as bad as Loveless's crime. She will return Worthy's love if he will no longer ask what she cannot grant. When Worthy threatens rape, Amanda escapes; and she returns only when he begs her forgiveness. Worthy's soliloquy, approving her purity and accepting her terms, ends the scene.

Scene 5 brings the serious and comic actions together at Lord Foppington's for the denouement. Although the occasion is intended to celebrate her marriage, Hoyden agrees with Nurse that Tom Fashion will make a better husband than Lord Foppington.

When Loveless, Foppington, and entourage arrive, Loveless reins in his desires so far as to refuse Foppington's offer of Hoyden as a mistress and to declare his fondness for Amanda. After a musical masque, Tom Fashion arrives to claim his bride, presents Nurse and Bull as witnesses, receives Sir Tunbelly's curse, and accepts Lord Foppington's reluctant congratulations with Hoyden on his arm.

Vanbrugh was acutely aware that, because of his haste in writing, the plot of *The Relapse* was lacking in unity and marred by improbable coincidences and faults in character motivation. There are, however, more incongruities in the comedy than Vanbrugh realized when he acknowledged them in his "Vindication." Most of them are incidental signs of inattention; others, like the coincidence of Loveless's falling in love with Amanda's cousin and the opportune arrival of Sir John Friendly, are easily overlooked in the acted play. Perhaps the most severe strain on the audience's credulity comes in Act I, scene 1, with the "indispensable" business that takes Loveless to London. His business could have been explained, but Vanbrugh does not do so; therefore, we are left wondering what sort of affair must be so important that it will lead Loveless to test his new-found virtue and that will allow Amanda to acquiesce in his decision.

Another weakness in probability comes with Amanda's lack of motivation in inviting Berinthia to stay with her, especially when it means exposing her husband to a pretty woman during his time of testing. Loveless's admiration for Berinthia leads to still another incongruity in his soliloquy (Act III, scene 2), where he must be expected to reveal his true thoughts: he confesses that Berinthia is the "only one on earth" for him; yet minutes later Amanda reports that he has been flirting with other women. It is incongruous, too, that in Act V, scene 2, Amanda would listen to praise of Loveless's new mistress without suspecting Berinthia, especially when her cousin describes her as "about my height; and very well shap'd" and "as straight as I am."

A final incongruity deserves special attention because it is at once a stage convention and an improbability. Elmer Stoll says of the sort of secret marriage that Chaplain Bull performs: "The hurried and huddled ceremonies, without licenses or once asking of the banns, by anybody in a wig, spectacles, and cassock, ought to have deceived nobody."[20] According to G. S. Alleman, Hoyden could have been released from her illegal marriage to Young Fashion; Bull could have been fined and suspended from holy orders for three years; and Tom could have been imprisoned "for taking away an unmarried woman under sixteen without the consent of her parents or guardians," as Lord Foppington knew ("He does deserve to be *chartré*, stap my Vitals.") (I, 77). The greater danger was that Sir Tunbelly could prove that Tom had used force, a capital offense.[21] But Restoration audiences seem to have accepted such marriages on the stage and, as with the coincidences noted earlier, would have overlooked the peculiarities of this one.

Vanbrugh's greater concern about the plot was that its double nature would prove to be a weakness. "I don't pretend, however, to have observ'd the nicety of Rule in this Play" (I, 209). It was written in haste, he pointed out in his "Vindication," and contained mistakes. But, he argued, there is much to be said against observing the rules too closely and "crowding a Comedy with a great deal of Intricate Plot" (I, 209). Congreve's masterpiece, *The Way of the World*, for example, was to suffer popular disapproval less than two years later for having a too complicated plot. Vanbrugh's story, as a matter of fact, was so neatly divided into two parts that the two sets of characters hardly met, and readers have disagreed as to which is the main and which the subplot. Some have seen Tom Fashion's victory as holding most of our interest;[22] and Collier's insistence that the Lord Foppington story was the main plot angered Vanbrugh because it was clearly less moral than that of Loveless and Amanda, and it was the morality of *The Relapse* that Vanbrugh was trying to demonstrate. "In short;" Vanbrugh argued, "My Lord *Foppington*, and the *Bridegroom*, and the *Bride*, and the *Justice*, and the *Matchmaker*, and the *Nurse*, and the *Parson* at the rear of 'em, are the Inferior Persons of the Play (I mean as to their business), and what they do, is more to divert the Audience, by something particular and whimsical in their Humours, than to instruct 'em in any thing that may be drawn from their Morals; though several useful things may in passing be pickt up from 'em too" (I, 210). And, he concluded, the main plot is "something of so much greater Importance than *Young Fashion's* marrying Miss *Hoyden*, that if I had call'd it the *Younger Brother*, or the *Fortunate Cheat*, instead of *The Relapse, or Virtue in Danger*, I had been just as much in the wrong, as Mr. *Collier* is now" (I, 213).

In choosing a double design for the action of his play, as he did, Vanbrugh was remaining true to an old tradition in the English theater. "A single intrigue in love," the character Courtall had said in Etherege's *She Wou'd if She Cou'd* (1668), "is as dull as a single plot in a play, and will tire a lover worse than t'other does an audience." But Vanbrugh was also aware that the theater audience was composed of a mixture of citizens and of wits and that his two stories gave additional opportunities for pleasing both. Two plots enabled him to increase the number of crises, and the rapid changing of scene gave the comedy a spirit of Shakespearean vivacity that was an added delight.

A stage direction in *The Confederacy*, Vanbrugh's translation of Dancourt (1705), indicates well how quickly the many necessary scene changes in *The Relapse* were made.[23] Act V opens in Gripe's house and after some dialogue among five of the characters, the apron is left bare, whereupon the "Scene Opens" to reveal Araminta, Corinna, Gripe, and others at tea. In a few moments Mr. Clip the goldsmith is announced and asks to speak with Gripe in the next room. The stage direction then reads, "They come forward, and the Scene shuts behind them." Both scene changes were accomplished with a downstage pair of sliding flats that were moved in grooves from either side of the proscenium arch until they met center stage so as to provide appropriate background for the action. Additional flats upstage extended part way onto the stage to create a sense of depth and to allow for exits and entrances, and several more pairs of closing flats upstage made possible rapid scene changes.

In *The Relapse*, for example, three rapid scene shifts in Act III made use of sliding flats. The garden scene would have been changed to Sir Tunbelly's country house with the closing of the downstage flats nearest the audience. In Scene 3, Tom and Lory's arrival at Tunbelly's gates would have been played on the large apron directly in front of the audience. Then the downstage flats would have opened to reveal Hoyden's room depicted on upstage flats. At her exit with Nurse, the upstage flats would have opened to Sir Tunbelly's hall; and he and Tom would have come forward to the audience, thus giving to the hall an air of spaciousness.

III *The Characters of the Main Plot*

By relegating the plot to a position of secondary importance, as he did, Vanbrugh was able to turn his attention in "Vindication" to the characters whom he considered to be the main source of the entertainment. "I believe I cou'd shew," he wrote, "that the chief entertainment, as well as the Moral, lies much more in the Characters and the Dialogue, than in the Business and the Event" (I, 209). As we have seen, Vanbrugh was inspired to write by contemplating the possibility that Loveless's reformation in Cibber's play might not be a permanent one: Loveless

appear'd to me to be got into so agreeable a Tract of Life, that I often took a pleasure to indulge a musing Fancy, and suppose myself in his place. The Happiness I saw him possest of, I lookt upon as a Jewel of a very great worth, which naturally lead me to the fear of losing it; I therefore consider'd by what Enemies 'twas most likely to be attack'd, and that directed me in the Plan of the Works that were most probable to defend it. I saw but one danger in Solitude and Retirement, and I saw a thousand in the bustle of the World; I therefore in a moment determin'd for the Countrey, and supposed *Loveless* and *Amanda* gone out of town (I, 211).

. . .

Loveless, He's so thoroughly wean'd from the taste of his Debauches, he has not a thought toward the Stage where they us'd to be acted. 'Tis Business, not Pleasure, brings him thither again, and his Wife can't persuade him there's the least danger of a Relapse; He's proud to think on what a Rock his Reformation is built, and resolves She herself shall be a Witness, that though the Winds blow, and the Billows roar, yet nothing can prevail against it (I, 211).

The test of Loveless's reformation comes, Vanbrugh continues, when he purposely goes to the playhouse. The woman he sees there is a temptation almost greater than he can resist, but he "despises her charms," has not a whit of desire for her, and is certain he loves no one but Amanda. When Berinthia comes to live with her cousin, however, "The battery is so near, there's no standing the Shot, Constancy's beaten down; the Breach is made, Resolution gives ground, and the Town's taken" (I, 212). In short, Propinquity is the villain, the "Frailty of Mankind" is the victim, and the moral is that not even the steadiest guard can keep out temptation.

Loveless's downward course begins in the first scene, when, after asserting that man's happiness is in his mind, he is led in the ensuing conversation with Amanda to the thought that death must end all of man's pleasure: "A bitter Pill it is to all; but doubles its ungrateful Taste,/ When Lovers are to swallow it" (I, 20). If there is a motive that drives him to betray Amanda, it is to be found here. His later seduction of Berinthia is done for no other reason than self-gratification, but it is the urge to gratify self intensified by the thought of man's transitory existence. Loveless may think of himself

as a Stoic, but he lacks the true self-knowledge that would enable
him to rise both above mere external circumstances and above the
thought of death.[24] Vanbrugh thus reveals Loveless to be a Hobbesian libertine rather than a Stoic, even before he has gazed upon
Berinthia and has succumbed to her charms.

Thomas Hobbes, whose skeptical philosophy Vanbrugh seems to
have read and admired, had considered man's life to be a succession
of passions that must be satisfied. Hobbes did not subscribe, therefore, to the absence of passion which the Stoic attained through
careful abstinence or even to the Epicurean's attainment of the
absence of pain through moderately indulged desires; for Hobbes,
instead, satiety was the continual fulfilling of one passion after
another until death ended all. To follow nature, Hobbes believed,
was to follow pleasure and to avoid pain. Loveless's second soliloquy
(Act III, scene 2) demonstrates what Hobbes would call De-
liberation—thought that is developed by conflicting responses to a
stimulus;[25] for Loveless is passionately attracted to Berinthia, but he
is grateful to Amanda and—as the next scene with Berinthia
indicates—he would not risk the loss of his present course of life for
momentary indulgence:

> LOVELESS. You might betray my Distemper to my Wife.
> BERINTHIA. And so lose all my Practice.
> LOV. Will you then keep my Secret?
> BER. I will, if it don't burst me.
> LOV. Swear.
> (I, 51)

If Loveless can achieve his desire in secret, all scruples disappear;
and his decision to pursue Berinthia is therefore the predictable
course for a low-minded libertine. However, there is irony in his
belief that he is master of his own passions; and it reaches its sharp-
est delineation at the beginning of Act II when he deprecates as
empty all the entertainments of the town but two: "Yet some there
are we may speak kindlier of: There are Delights, (of which a private
Life is destitute) which may divert an honest Man, and be a harm-
less Entertainment to a virtuous Woman. The Conversation of the
Town is one; and truly, (with some small Allowances) the Plays, I
think, may be esteem'd another" (I, 32). Ironically, Loveless first
sees Berinthia at a play; and it is doubly ironic that the play depicts
the relapse of one like himself. It is also ironic that much of the

conversation that we hear on the stage concerns little more than bawdy, fashions, marriages of convenience, and speculations about intrigue.

Loveless lacks self-knowledge, but Amanda is not entirely free of ignorance about her own nature. She believes in the superiority of the will over the passions; but, in her soliloquy (Act V, Scene 4), she finds herself strangely tempted to revenge herself upon her husband. Her virtue, said Vanbrugh in the "Vindication,"

> looks so Sacred, one wou'd think no Mortal durst approach it; and seems so fix'd one wou'd believe no Engine cou'd shake it: Yet loosen one Stone, the Weather works in, and the Structure molders apace to decay. She discovers her Husband's return to his Inconstancy. The unsteadiness of his Love gives her a Contempt of his Person; and what lessens her Opinion, declines her Inclination. As her Passion for him is abated, that against him's inflam'd; and as her Anger increases, her Reason's confus'd. Her Judgment in disorder, her Religion's unhing'd; and that Fence being broken, she lies widely expos'd . . . (I, 212–13).

A reading of the play does not support, however, Vanbrugh's insistence upon the imminence of Amanda's fall: she appears to us more weatherworthy than his metaphor suggests. Although her name means "loving" or "affectionate," she clearly embodies the "Natural Coldness," as Congreve put it, that the era accepted as characteristic of womankind.[26] And, in her final scene with Worthy, it is not to prevent his seduction that she prays to Heaven and Virtue but to prevent his Rape.

What Vanbrugh has most successfully accomplished in Amanda, rather than merely to dramatize her near fall, is to portray in her a virtue whose basis is not ignorance but full knowledge of the ways of the world. Whether we see her as a continuation of Cibber's Amanda, whose brief life with Loveless and long "widowhood" in London had sharpened her perception of the human condition, it is clear from the opening scene of *The Relapse* that she is no country wife, no Prue or Hoyden who is to be seduced by the first sweet-smelling peruke. As well as Vanbrugh seems to have known his John Milton, it is not too far-fetched to see her as a dramatic example of the well-known passage in *Areopagitica:* "I cannot praise a fugitive and cloistered virtue, unexercised and unbreathed, that never sallies out and sees her adversary, but slinks out of the race, where that immortal garland is to be run for, not without dust and heat."[27]

That Amanda's virtue is not cloistered is made clear in a number
of passages throughout the play. She warns Loveless repeatedly that
their trip to the city involves dangers. "Men find out softer ways to
quench their Fires," she tells him (I, 20). "The strongest Vessels, if
they put to Sea,/ May possibly be lost" (I, 20). Once in London, she
reminds him of the "loose obscene encouragement to Vice" in the
plays; and she is quick to see that his gazing upon a pretty woman
with "eager eyes" is a sign that he is in danger. But Amanda is not so
prudish that she cannot tease Lord Foppington about his intrigues
or Berinthia about her lovers. "Why is it possible," she asks Berinthia, "that one so Young and Beautiful as you, shou'd live and have
no Secrets?"

> BERINTHIA. What Secrets do you mean?
> AMANDA. Lovers.
> BER. O Twenty; but not one secret one amongst 'em. Lovers in this Age
> have too much Honour to do any thing under-hand; they do all above-
> board.
> AMAN. That now methinks wou'd make me hate a Man (I, 42).

Amanda's questions to Berinthia, however, are not entirely in jest;
she is too wise a general not to wish to know the disposition of the
enemy's forces, both those that threaten Loveless and those that
threaten her. Amanda's invitation to her cousin Berinthia to live
with her may not be sufficiently motivated, to be sure, but we may
speculate that Vanbrugh intended it to arise from Amanda's desire
to learn from Berinthia more about her own dangers, especially any
that might be posed by a man whose reputation for discretion had
been established in *Love's Last Shift*. There is, however, little to
support Vanbrugh's contention in the "Vindication" that Amanda
sees Worthy as "a Comforter in her Afflictions," that "she desires
the Physician may be always in her sight," and that she "grows
pleas'd with his Person as well as his Advice" (I, 213). In his reply to
Collier, Vanbrugh was hard pressed to defend the morality of the
play and, in particular, to demonstrate that Loveless's betrayal of
Amanda and her near fall serve as a warning to husbands. In trying
to make his reply to Collier, Vanbrugh committed an understandable exaggeration.

Worthy's attempted seduction of Amanda fails because she
has firmly resolved not to cuckold Loveless, even when she has full

knowledge not only of his relapse but also of her means to attain revenge. It is not merely her doubt about Worthy's sincerity (although she has it) but her faith that is the source of the strength that enables her to resist the revenge he offers.[28] Her resolution is clearly seen in her soliloquy just before Worthy's arrival: "I still have Darts, and I can shoot 'em too; / They're not so blunt, but they can enter still; /The Want's not in my Power, but in my Will" (I, 90). In contrast to Loveless's Stoic self-confidence, Amanda's Christianity is cognizant of the power of passion and the weakness of reason. But, at the same time, she believes that the will can find strength in prayer, as her prayers to heaven before and during the attempted rape illustrate, and as her "repentance" exchange with Worthy concludes:

WORTHY. What must I do to be forgiven by you?
AMANDA. Repent, and never more offend.
WOR. Repentance for past Crimes, is just and easie; but sin no more's a Task too hard for Mortals.
AMAN. Yet those who hope for Heaven, must use their best endeavours to perform it.
WOR. Endeavours we may use, but Flesh and Blood are got in t'other Scale; and they are pondrous things.
AMAN. Whate'er they are; there is a Weight in Resolution sufficient for their Ballance. The Soul, I do confess, is usually so careless of its Charge, so soft, and so indulgent to desire, it leaves the Reins in the wild Hand of Nature, who, like a Phaeton, drives the fiery Chariot, and sets the World on Flame. Yet still the Sovereignty is in the Mind, whene'er it pleases to exert its Force (I, 92–93).

The strong impression we receive, in this last scene as in Amanda's earlier speeches, is that of a well-tested virtue, based on knowledge of the world and rigorously defended, and not, as has sometimes been asserted, on the goodness like that in sentimental comedy, easily attained and abundantly rewarded. For Amanda, virtue must be its own reward.

In some ways Worthy's conversion presents a much greater challenge to our credulity than that of Cibber's Loveless. Worthy is, after all, much more a man of brains than is Loveless who is a creature of passion in both plays. The redemption of Cibber's Loveless, we recall, comes after ten years of debauchery when he is impoverished and friendless. Vanbrugh's Worthy, on the other

hand, has no such external forces operating on him to make him
abandon his attempt to seduce Amanda; he is entirely persuaded by
her arguments for adhering to virtue. Cibber's Loveless and Vanbrugh's Worthy, it is true, both qualify their reformation. Cibber's
character ecstatically lauds the rapture of virtuous love; but, as we
have already noticed, his happiness will last, as he says, only as long
as he is in Amanda's embrace. Vanbrugh's Worthy, on the other
hand, is much more conscious of his weakness and more direct in
expressing it. "How long this influence may last," he says, "Heaven
knows. But in this moment of my purity, I cou'd on her own terms,
accept her Heart. . . . When Truth's extorted from us, then we own
[that] the Robe of Vertue is a graceful Habit" (I, 93).

Worthy's conversion, however, is not entirely incredible; it is not
the "inept about-face" that Paul Mueschke and Jeannette Fleisher
charge.[29] In the play that served as Vanbrugh's model, Cibber had
assigned the usual identifying name to a character whom he conceived to be essentially good. In spite of his part in tricking
Wisewoud, the Elder Worthy in Love's Last Shift impresses us to be
the man of philosophical restraint that his very first speech reveals.
Vanbrugh accepted the Cibber model for Worthy, just as he accepted the basic character traits of Amanda and Loveless. If Worthy
is a libertine, as the Younger Worthy hints, he is far more discreet
than his brothers Horner and Dorimant; but, like them, his name
announces him to be capable of acting precisely as he does.

The distinct image that we gain of Vanbrugh's Worthy is that of
the traditional Restoration rake whose libertinism is much tempered
by self-control but whose coolly detached intellect is enlivened by
an emotional response to the "food of angels" that Amanda provides.
Amanda's part in Worthy's temporary conversion is to rely upon his
self-control and to arouse that awareness of the divine that he be-
latedly discovers in himself.[30] The conversion is neither so abrupt
nor so permanent as that in many a Heroic tragedy, but it still places
Vanbrugh ultimately on the side of the angels because, at the same
time that he shows the fall of Loveless, he depicts the conversion of
a better man—one who is much closer to the Restoration ideal of
intellect and self-control.[31]

Most troublesome of all the characters, of course, is Berinthia,
Worthy's lieutenant in the campaign to seduce Amanda. She has
been ranked with the basest of Restoration female characters, and
Vanbrugh himself summarily dismisses her in "Vindication" as an

example of evil human conduct. The best he can say in Berinthia's defense is that such things as she are to be found and that "she's brought upon the Stage to Ridicule something that's off on't" (I, 202). Like Iago, however, she challenges our understanding of human motivation. From scene to scene we watch her sink more deeply into deceit and depravity; yet we find her insights into human nature and her occasional frankness to be refreshing, and we are left at the end of the play with the uncomfortable feeling that either we or the poet have overlooked something in her character.

The chief point at issue, as Jeremy Collier shrewdly observed, is that Berinthia is a female libertine who is neither dressed in hypocritical honor to arouse our ridicule nor clad in satanic viciousness to evoke our horror. At one and the same time that she tempts Loveless, she endeavors to debauch his wife by pimping for Worthy; but she acts from no diabolical design of revenge or from ambition. She does what she does because she enjoys sex and mistrusts marriage and because she sees the campaign against Amanda's virtue as exercising "almost all the entertaining faculties of a woman." Although there is a spirit of independence about Berinthia as well as a sharp wit and an ability to read the motives of others that arouses our admiration or at least our toleration, we see in her, as she sees in herself, all the failings of her sex—hypocrisy, invention, deceit, flattery, mischief, and lying.

Unlike many another lady libertine of Restoration comedy, however, Berinthia has been provided with understandable motives. While still very young, she had been forced by a mother she feared to marry a man she did not love. Her wedded life had been miserable until her husband's death, and from it she had drawn the conclusion that the majority of men are driven to marriage only by lust and by love of conquest. "Nature has made them Children," she says, "and us Babies. Now, *Amanda*, how we us'd our Babies, you may remember. We were mad to have 'em, as soon as we saw 'em; kist 'em to pieces, as soon as we got 'em; then pull'd off their Cloaths, saw 'em naked, and so threw 'em away" (I, 83). The wit in her words conceals the depth of her unhappiness, for she and her husband had at last agreed on nothing. "We were dull Company at Table, worse Abed. Whenever we met, we gave one another the Spleen. And never agreed but once, which was about lying alone" (I, 45). Because of the misery of her marriage, she has now constructed an ideal of a man; and she has made it an article of her faith that there

are such things as star-crossed lovers. Berinthia's philosophy of love
is thus far more romantic than Amanda's, for it argues that, when a
"man of brains" has found his true love, he will be faithful to her
(although rare is the man who finds her). Amanda, more practically,
sees that a man may have a true love, stray on occasion for mere
variety, but return again.

In the last analysis, the uncertainty about Berinthia's character—our inability to accept her as primarily good or as primarily
evil—prevents the famous seduction episode in Act IV from achiev-
ing the comic success that it is sometimes credited with having.[32]
There are none of the witty double entendres of the china scene in
The Country Wife, for example, and little of the incongruous that is
otherwise the stuff of comedy. The scene may deserve applause, as
William Hazlitt insisted, for the skill with which Vanbrugh ac-
complishes an advance in the action of the play;[33] but there is little
more than Berinthia's *very soft* and very hypocritical call for help
that deserves laughter.

IV *"The Inferior Persons"*

The characters of the comic subplot, whom Vanbrugh called in
the "Vindication" the "Inferior Persons of the Play," are led by his
triumphant comic creation Lord Foppington. Cibber, to be sure,
had provided in Sir Novelty Fashion a superb base on which to
build—especially Fashion's self-conscious foppery, incongruously
crude oaths, and elaborate self-praise. But what is seen only in
outline form in Cibber's fop is fleshed out—as it were—in Vanbrugh's. The oaths and the pronunciation become a trademark
rather than a mere accoutrement, and they provide such instances
of outrageous humor as that in Vanbrugh's duel scene (I, 39):[34]

LORD FOPPINGTON. (to Amanda, squeezing her hand) I am in love with
you to Desperation, *strike me speechless* (italics added).
AMANDA. (Giving him a box on the ear) Then thus I return your passion;
An impudent Fool!

When Loveless and Foppington fight and the latter is wounded:

LORD FOPPINGTON. (falling back, and leaning upon his sword.) Ah—quite
thro' the Body—*Stap my Vitals* (italics added).

The famous sketch in *The Relapse*, Act II, scene i, of Lord Foppington's life—a brilliant postmortem on the corpse of a beau—has
its origin in *Love's Last Shift* in Fashion's courting scene with Narcissa where Sir Novelty catalogues his accomplishments in the world
of stylish dress as an encouragement to Narcissa's love: "Why,
Madam, don't you think it more Glory to be beloved by one eminently particular Person, whom all the Town knows and talks of;
than to be ador'd by five hundred dull Souls that have lived incog-
nito?"[35] But where Sir Novelty Fashion's self-outline is brief and
lacking in comic complexity, Lord Foppington's is rich in uncon-
scious irony and is developed at length: "Far example, Madam, my
Life; my Life, Madam, is a perpetual Stream of Pleasure, that glides
thro' such a Variety of Entertainments, I believe the wisest of our
Ancestors never had the least Conception of any of 'em" (I, 37). His
typical day, of course, consists of nothing more exciting than rising
at ten, walking in the park or being in the chocolate-houses until
dinner, and from there to the theater. After the play, he gives an
hour to leading the ladies to their carriages, four hours to drinking,
and eight to sleeping. And the next day follows the same dull pattern.

The chief difference, however, between Cibber's creation and
Vanbrugh's is that Lord Foppington's conscious effort to be the
coxcombs' leader because they are "so prevailing a party" takes on a
note of seriousness not found in Cibber. The self-centered
harmlessness displayed so gracefully by Sir Novelty Fashion and his
original, Sir Fopling Flutter, is transformed in Vanbrugh's character
into self-centered viciousness. Sir Novelty, for example, had
paraded only his foppishness in the "courting scene" of *Love's Last
Shift*. In the comparable scene of *The Relapse*, however, Lord Foppington established a powerful undercurrent of tension by announcing in an aside upon his arrival: "Dear *Loveless*, I am overjoy'd to
see you have brought your Family to Tawn again; I am, stap my
Vitals—[*Aside*.] Far I design to lye with your Wife" (I, 36). A similar
increase in tension is apparent when we compare, for example, Sir
Fopling Flutter's famous entrance with Lord Foppington's dressing
scene. The former is a mild satire about overdressing, a delicate
catalogue of affectation; the latter, however, while an effective ridiculing of foppery, takes on a new and painful dimension because of
Tom's presence. The penniless younger brother stands by, ignored
and embarrassed, while the elder—already having spent ten

thousand pounds to purchase a title—quibbles with his wigmaker about the number of hairs in his elaborate peruke.

The character that Foppington represents, said Vanbrugh, is designed to arouse the contempt of the audience. Unlike his brother fops, however, Lord Foppington is a fool by design rather than by nature; he is a potential true wit run mad rather than a true witwoud. As Congreve put it—in his letter to John Dennis the year before—"*Humour* is from Nature, *Habit* from Custom, and *Affectation* from Industry."[36] Foppington's absurd life of pleasure is deliberately designed,[37] and his social climbing is an obvious satire on the excessively diligent striving of the English middle class. Like many of his fellow comic dramatists, Vanbrugh saw a strange and unwelcome change coming in English society as the moneyed class began to replace the landed gentry as the repository of political power. What was even more unacceptable was the fact that it was possible for middle class wealth to buy its way into the nobility.[38] Hence the type of Lord Foppington could not fail to be a success with both audiences of the late seventeenth century—the nobility who feared the encroachment of wealth upon their traditional sphere and the sensible among the citizens who saw in Foppington's purchase of a title a foolish expenditure of good English money.

The comic success of Lord Foppington, then, lies in the changes Vanbrugh made in his original. By elevating him to the peerage, the playwright opened an entirely new vein of humor. By giving him more intelligence and more wit than his brothers, by turning his oaths and his pronunciation into identifying traits, and by adding to his foolishness a new dimension of vice, Vanbrugh reinforced the seriousness of the main plot and created a character more memorable than his antecedents. For Lytton Strachey, as a matter of fact, Lord Foppington is almost heroic: "With his delicious absurdities, his preposterous airs and graces, his blood-curdling oaths and lackadaisical pronunciation, yet [he] manages to be incessantly witty, to dominate whatever company he may be in, and, in fact, in some strange way, to be great. Vanbrugh, with true English humour, has resisted the temptation of making an utter fool of his fool, and has shown us, even in that strutting clothes-block, the eminence of the human spirit."[39]

Within less than a decade after his creation, however, Lord Foppington was to become little more than villainous. In Cibber's *The Careless Husband* (1704), he degenerates into a calculating whore-master, a brutal husband who has married only to pay his debts and to disinherit his younger brother. It was a melancholy decline, and Vanbrugh must have mourned his hero's decay as much as Addison was to regret the sad change that Steele had wrought in Sir Roger de Coverley.

Second only to Lord Foppington among the characters of the comic subplot is Tom Fashion, his younger brother. In "Vindication," of course, Vanbrugh had protested against Collier's charge that Tom was the playwright's favorite character. But we cannot take seriously Vanbrugh's explanation that, because Tom's new country wife is "likely to make his heart ake," Tom Fashion's trickery brings him no reward. Vanbrugh likes Tom, has lavished much care upon his development, and clearly does not see his young hero as much concerned about the success of his marriage when he has Hoyden's fortune. "Get but the House," Tom tells Lory; "let the Devil take the Heiress, I say" (I, 57).

Nevertheless, Young Fashion possesses a moral nature rare among Restoration stage types. Not only is Tom Vanbrugh's best original contribution to the inherited Loveless-Amanda plot, but he is also new in other important ways. He is the first anti-hero to appear in Restoration comedy; for he is so ground down by poverty that he is forced to defraud a poor waterman; he is virtually inarticulate in the presence of his haughty, witty brother; he is forced by circumstances to accept the services of the loathesome Coupler; and he is nearly trapped by Foppington and the enraged Clumsey when his shift fails. Yet, in the end, he wins the girl and—of more moment—the two thousand pounds a year. Furthermore, he does so without losing his conscience. Although Tom finds himself in the familiar comic situation of the gallant with a ready way to gull a witwoud brother and a country bumpkin his moral scruples at betraying Lord Foppington, his ability to see the conflict between conscience and necessity, mark him as an exception to the rule for younger brother rakes. He is too proud to beg or flatter, but he is too aware of the gross injustice of his brother's rejection of him to maintain an overly nice conscience.

Just as Vanbrugh's treatment of Tom as a man about town is unique in Restoration comedy, so is the situation in which Tom finds himself. In his extensive reading of seventeenth century comedies, Frank M. Patterson has found no precedent for the kind of trick that Young Fashion employs in order to marry a fortune. In like manner,

Vanbrugh seems to have been the first to explore sympathetically
the predicament of the younger brother at the end of the century
when changes in custom and in law had, in general, resulted in the
disinheriting of younger sons and the assigning of the entire estate
to the eldest.[40] It is possible, of course, that, as he began to write in
January 1696, Captain Vanbrugh found a convenient model for the
elder-younger brother conflict in the most popular comedy of the
preceding season, Congreve's Love for Love. In it, however, the
rakish elder son (Valentine) was penniless and importunate; and the
younger son (Ben) enjoyed his father's favor. It is likely, as well, that
Vanbrugh—himself an older brother with younger brothers of
whom he was unusually fond—saw the dramatic excitement possible
if the close relationship between the two Worthy brothers in Cibber's Love's Last Shift could be disrupted and the advantage given
to the younger. Congreve's play and Vanbrugh's experience both
had a part in the genesis of Young Tom Fashion.

The minor characters of the comic subplot can be assigned to
three groups: those—like the Waterman, Lory, and Coupler—who
belong to Tom; those associated with Foppington; and those who
belong to the Clumsey household. Alone among the first two groups
as sufficiently unusual to demand our attention is old Coupler, the
homosexual matchmaker who contrives the plot to trick Sir Tunbelly
Clumsey. There are relatively few references to homosexuality, of
course, in Restoration comedy; but the problem began to arouse
interest about the turn of the century with the increase in musical
influences from Italy, where the vice was supposed to flourish.
Among the playwrights who had at least suggested the "Italian vice"
before Vanbrugh were Thomas Otway, Aphra Behn, Thomas Southerne, Thomas Dilke, and George Granville.

Dilke's comedy The Lover's Luck, with its scene between
Goosandelo and Jocond, and Granville's The She-Gallants, both
performed at Lincoln's Inn Fields the month before Vanbrugh
began to write, may have given him the idea for including a character with homosexual tendencies. And he may have found the model
for a bawd with such tendencies in the character of Sir Jolly Jumble
in Otway's The Soldier's Fortune (1681).[41] But, on the whole,
Coupler is an original Vanbrugh creation; he is frank and realistic in
his dealings with Tom; he is bold in his scheming, and he is as full of
confidence in his ability to control others as Alexander the Great, to
whom he compares himself.

Like the serious plot of *The Relapse*, the comic subplot has as its mainspring the problem of marriage; and the minor characters of the Clumsey household are entirely motivated to act by desires that relate in some way to matrimony. Sir Tunbelly's only goal is to form a connection with a noble family, and he has arranged what amounts to the virtual purchase of Lord Foppington as a son-in-law in order to attain it. So clearly has Clumsey visualized the rewards of such an alliance—the impressive wedding ceremony as well as the fame of the name—that he rejects with contempt the pretended bridegroom's suggestion that a simple ceremony would save money. But the blunt country frankness that he exhibits in his talk about the wedding, his convivial coarseness, and the farcical elements of the scenes in which he appears keep him from turning the corner into dramatic seriousness. There is never any danger that filial ingratitude will make him a Lear. Just as Foppington's purchase of a title was laughable because it wasted good money, so Sir Tunbelly's aspirations must have been seen by both the wits and the good burghers in Vanbrugh's audience as a comic warning against the growing practice of marriage for social and economic advantage.

While Sir Tunbelly Clumsey is eager to forge an alliance with a noble family, his daughter Hoyden is eager for an alliance with any man: "Sure never no body was us'd as I am," she says at her first appearance on stage. "I know well enough what other Girls do, for all they think to make a Fool of me: It's well I have a Husband a coming, or Icod, I'd marry the Baker, I wou'd so" (I, 59). Her character is reflected in her name, Hoyden: she is high-spirited, impudent, boisterous; and, as Hazlitt observed, "a fine bouncing piece of flesh and blood."[42] She is not likely, however, to prove a constant wife or—if we may speculate further—a very happy one. The gap between Hoyden and Berinthia is not wide: the country wife will not be far behind her city cousin, and will—as Tom Fashion predicts—"prove a *March* Hare all the year round. . . . Hey to the Park and the Play, and the Church, and the Devil; she'll shew 'em sport I'll warrant 'em" (I, 63). Like Congreve's Prue of the season before, and like Mrs. Pinchwife of Wycherley's *The Country Wife* (1675), Hoyden belongs to that small but lively class of Restoration heroines whose innocence is exceeded only by their eagerness to lose it.

Much of the picture that Vanbrugh draws of Hoyden is indebted, as Collier suggested, to Tom D'Urfey's trilogy *The Comical History*

of Don Quixote and the character of Mary the Buxom, Sancho's
daughter and a coarse and boisterous peasant girl. In Part I (performed in May 1694), D'Urfey had described her as "a Rude, laughing, clownish Hoyden"; in Part II (also in May 1694), she is called "a
ramping ill-bred Dowdy" and is given three scenes; and in each her
boisterousness and her "countrylike" talk are her chief traits. In Part
III, in which Mary's marriage is the central comic action, she delivers a prologue in which she charges that there are other "Hoydens"
and then proceeds to describe the country wife who goes to town to
buy new clothes and to go to plays; there she "hoydens with the
men, / Cuckolds her Spouse, and so Romps down ag'en." Although
Mary the Buxom is more vulgar in her conduct and more country in
her talk, she clearly provided the name and the character outline for
Vanbrugh's Hoyden.

The key to the success or failure of Tom's plan to marry Hoyden is
Chaplain Bull, Sir Tunbelly's priest and the source of boundless
irritation to Jeremy Collier. Bull marries Tom and Hoyden without
banns or license when Tom assures him that a fat living will be his
reward. But Bull also conceals this first marriage from Sir Tunbelly
and is ready to perform a second between Lord Foppington and
Hoyden when Tom's imposture is disclosed. "I do confess," Bull
argues, "to take two Husbands for the satisfaction of the Flesh, is to
commit the Sin of Exorbitancy; but to do it for the Peace of the
Spirit, is no more than to be drunk by way of Physick . . ." (I, 78).
The treatment that Captain Vanbrugh dealt to men of the cloth in
this way was harsh but comically effective. Such satire is justifiable
when excesses exist, and England in 1696 had more than its share of
secular priests. At the very time that Bull was first taking the stage,
Jonathan Swift was beginning his savage satire on clerical folly in *A
Tale of a Tub;* and a dozen years later Pope would speak for all
reasonable men in defending Roger Bull as a true picture of clerical
excess: "Priests indeed in their Character, as they represent God,
are sacred; . . . but you will own a great many of 'em are very odd
fellows & the devil a bit of Likeness in 'em. Yet I do assure you, I
honor the good as much as I detest the bad, & I think that in
condemning these, we praise those. I am so far from esteeming ev'n
the worst unworthy of my Protection, that I have defended their
character (in Congreve's and Vanbrook's Plays) even against their
own Brethren. . . ."[43]

Along with Chaplain Bull in the adventure of the fraudulent marriage is Nurse, Vanbrugh's masterpiece in miniature; for she is a minor character who comes alive as fully as Shakespeare's Nurse in *Romeo and Juliet* and who in one or two scenes outdoes her Elizabethan counterpart. No brief scene in *The Relapse* comes closer to comic perfection than the vignette in which Nurse tells Tom of Hoyden's infancy:

NURSE. Alas, all I can boast of is, I gave her pure good Milk, and so your Honour wou'd have said, an you had seen how the poor thing suck't it—Eh, God's Blessing on the sweet Face on't; how it us'd to hang at this poor Tett, and suck and squeeze, and kick and sprawl it wou'd, till the Belly on't was so full, it wou'd drop off like a Leech.

HOYDEN. (To Nurse, taking her angrily aside.) Pray one word with you; prithee Nurse don't stand ripping up Old Stories, to make one asham'd before one's Love; do you think such a fine proper Gentleman as he, cares for a fiddlecome Tale of a draggle-tail'd Girl; . . . (I, 63).

Nothing could better demonstrate Vanbrugh's powers of observation and his genius for selecting from everyday life the substance of effective comedy.

V *The Moral of the Story*

In the preface to the published *Relapse*, Captain Vanbrugh had denied the charge of bawdy in his comedy; and, in his reply to Jeremy Collier's attack in the spring of 1698, he argued that all three of his plays were in general "a Discouragement to Vice and Folly; I am sure I intended it, and I hope I have performed it" (I, 195). The seriousness of Vanbrugh's claim is open to doubt, at least in regard to *The Relapse* and *The Provok'd Wife;* for *Aesop* had been too chaste, too charged with "downright dull instruction," as the prologue put it, to offend anybody. There are not, it is true, any obscene expressions upon the stage in *The Relapse*, but the seduction scene in Act IV is suggestive enough; and it ranks in indecency of action only slightly below that most infamous of bawdy scenes in Restoration comedy, the "China Scene" of Wycherley's *The Country Wife*. In addition, Worthy's attempted rape of Amanda seems intended to arouse the prurient interest of the audience; but its impact depended, of course, upon how the scene was acted. This factor makes it difficult to accept unequivocally Vanbrugh's conclu-

sion to "Vindication": "I was afraid the Rigor of the Moral wou'd
have damn'd the Play" (I, 215).

The chief point at issue in Vanbrugh's play, as in Restoration
comedy generally, is how to evaluate a kind of drama that is at once
moral and immoral, that simultaneously titillates and teaches. In
some Restoration comedy, as a matter of fact, like Wycherley's
Country Wife, the audience is not only presented with scenes that
encourage lasciviousness but is taught that hypocrisy is the only
indecency in adultery and fornication. "Of all the diversions that the
world has invented," wrote Pascal in *Pensées* when speaking of dangers to chaste living, "there is none to be feared more than the
comedy."[44]

On the opposite side of the argument are those who argue like
John Dennis that "the Play-House carries, or should carry, the An-
tidote with the Poison," or like T. S. Eliot, who lauds manners
comedy as eminently moral and who can find a word to speak in
favor even of bawdy. "The morality of our Restoration drama cannot
be impugned," says Eliot. "It assumes orthodox Christian morality,
and laughs (in its comedy) at human nature for not living up to it. It
retains its respect for the divine by showing the failure of the human." And later on, "We all like its indecency when it is really
witty, as it sometimes is."[45] The difficulty with either extreme point
of view is that neither one sufficiently recognizes the validity of its
opposing argument nor does either define satisfactorily all Restoration comedies. It is certainly not true of *The Relapse* that its major
trust is against chaste living; and it is true that Berinthia and Loveless enjoy their iniquity; but, in spite of the appeal to pruriency in
the comedy, it is Amanda's virtue that we admire, and its perfection
illuminates the grossness of Loveless's betrayal.

This is not to say, on the other hand, that Vanbrugh accepts
Christian morality as the sole standard for his comedy and that his
laughter is intended to bring straying black sheep back to the fold.
Rather, he aims satiric shafts at a variety of extremes in human
conduct—at the eccentric affectation of Foppington, at Lory's and
Nurse's overfamiliar attitude toward their betters, at the grossness
of Clumsey, at the blatant sexuality of Hoyden, and at the worldly
urges of Chaplain Bull. At the same time, Vanbrugh holds up for
emulation those whose virtue is enlightened by knowledge of the
world (Amanda), whose vice is tempered by Platonic idealism
(Worthy), and those (like Tom) whose Odyssean quick wit brings

victory over fate, foppish scoundrels, boorish social climbers, and fickle wives. If Berinthia alone escapes either censure or praise, it is because she presents for Vanbrugh an insoluble problem.

Like his predecessors in Restoration comedy, Vanbrugh was primarily interested in trying to make sense out of sexual relationships; but, unlike them, he turned nearly all of his attention to the sex problems of the married rather than to those of the unmarried. Whereas the chief concern of the belles and beaux who populated the stage of Etherege, Wycherley, and Congreve was to capture a mate or a mistress, Vanbrugh's characters struggle with the problem of what to do with a mate when one has one. An even more significant difference between Vanbrugh and his antecedents is his even-handed treatment of the sex combat; for, if the deck was heavily loaded in earlier plays on the side of the Restoration rake, Vanbrugh gives the lady a fair deal.

Whereas earlier comedy had pretended to treat woman as man's equal in wit and morality but had in fact exploited her, Captain Vanbrugh gave Amanda both sophistication *and* virtue; and he gave Berinthia intellect, will, appetite, and honesty equal to those of any Restoration rake and superior to many of its belles'. In Vanbrugh's *Relapse*, it is as if Etherege's witty and careless adolescents have passed into adulthood, some to grow hardened in vice, others to attain self-knowledge and even wisdom, and all to suffer the pains of making decisions for which they are now accountable. Dobrée puts the contrast well in his introduction to Vanbrugh's *Works:* "What to us seems to distinguish the people of Wycherley and Congreve from those of Vanbrugh is . . . that the two first groups seem to be acting under the sway of some compelling internal mechanism, which is replaced by free will in the characters of *The Relapse*. . ." (I, xv).

The stereotypes and stock situations that had prevailed in comedy until *The Relapse* now take on a new—and in some ways less comic—realism. Amanda triumphs in virtue; Berinthia persists in vice. One male libertine relapses; another reforms. Both aspects of the seventeenth century version of courtly love are satisfied with the assumption that woman is a semidivine creature whose virtue can transform her admirers and with the belief (expressed superbly by Constant in *The Provok'd Wife*, [Act III, scene i]) that true love or intense passion can only be found outside of marriage, that constancy "cannot buckle to the chains of wedlock." There is something in *The Relapse* for the romantic and something for the cynic, some-

thing for the ladies of the boxes and something for the gentlemen of
the pit, something for the Cavalier, and something for the Puritan
merchant. The realism of *The Relapse* is that of the Ibsenian problem drama more than that of Restoration comedy. Vanbrugh's great
gift is a sympathy that leads him to treat with understanding the
troubles of married life and the embarrassed suffering of the disin-
herited younger brother.

When realism is this much in balance, when widely differing
segments of society could find in *The Relapse* a point of view to
accept and characters with whom to identify, the possibilities for
comic action are severely limited. Comedy of manners is, after all,
dependent upon accepted social norms; we laugh for the most part
to reflect our disapproval of unsocial or antisocial behavior, of behavior that is either inappropriate or awkward according to some
identifiable and agreed-upon standard.

But the characters of the main plot cannot easily be found guilty of
conduct that is incongruous according to a standard accepted by the
most part of the audience. Loveless is by nature a libertine, and his
deviation into chastity is a foregone failure. Amanda is by nature a
précieuse, and she remains true to her semidivine character.
Worthy has the best of both worlds; like Etherege's Dorimant, he
has been momentarily converted by the love of a beautiful woman;
but there is more than a hint that his future life will not be entirely
virtuous. None of these is a comic treatment; the pit applauds Loveless and the boxes applaud Amanda; but both can find something to
approve in Worthy. Our laughter in *The Relapse* is instead at the
stock character of the fop—who tries too diligently to assume the
accoutrements of London civilization—and of the bumpkin who
makes no attempt at all.

In this judgment alone, the pit and boxes can agree; and, if the
resolution of *The Relapse* is unsatisfactory, it is a resolution that
accords with real life and not with romance. A final scene of affection
between Loveless and Amanda would have left the audience in an
agony of curiosity to know how an off-stage reconciliation could have
been effected. A show of antagonism between them would have
opened a new set of complications inappropriate for a last scene, and
it would have detracted from the denouement of the comic subplot.
The ending of *The Relapse* is closer to the way of the world than the
neat endings of most contemporaneous comedies. Reformations are
rare, relapses occur, moral victories are hard won and easily re-

versed, and human nature, in spite of John Locke, holds little promise of permanent improvement.

CHAPTER 4

The Provok'd Wife

T HE second and last of Captain John Vanbrugh's original comedies to be produced, although certainly the first to be composed, is *The Provok'd Wife;* and it is a much more traditional
Restoration comedy in its unity and in its display of witty conversation than *The Relapse*. Its central thesis, like that of its predecessor,
however, is that constancy in marriage is a tenuous thing since it
depends upon a human nature that is at best uncertain and at worst
perverse and upon an institution that appears more suited to discourage and even kill mutual love and respect than to preserve and
strengthen them.

In order to achieve his theme, Vanbrugh established two sets of
love triangles—a gross and quarrelsome husband with his wife,
Lady Brute, and her would-be lover, and a rakish misogynist who is
loved by two ladies. These six characters are related, in turn, to one
another as niece, friend, neighbor, and so on; but the relationships
never cause confusion in the acting or in the reading as is the case,
for example, in Congreve's incredibly complex *The Way of the
World*, in Vanbrugh's own *The Confederacy*, and in many another
Restoration comedy; and Lady Brute's temptation to revenge,
furthermore, is related in some way to all the other events in the
play. The denouement is similarly uncomplicated, hardly a denouement at all; for the young lovers are to be married—as we had
guessed all along—the lady fop is exposed; and the unhappily married couple is left—unhappily married.

I *The Plot*

Unlike *The Relapse*, *The Provok'd Wife* is an entirely original
play, composed over a very long period of time, and with a highly
unified plot in the classic sex-combat pattern of Restoration comedy.
It bears, perhaps, some distant relationships to George Etherege's

94

She Wou'd if She Cou'd (1668) and, as Curt Zimansky points out in his recent edition of *The Provok'd Wife*, to Thomas Otway's *The Soldier's Fortune* (1681) because of its character grouping of boorish husband, tempted wife, brisk niece, and so on. The double triangle in Vanbrugh's comedy, however, is more likely a coincidence than an evidence of influence. Given a quarrelsome husband and a provoked wife as a start (and Vanbrugh needed no creative genius to discover that combination), a seventeenth century playwright could be expected to add a spark for temptation (as Etherege had done), give the spark a comrade for conversation, give the comrade a girl relative of the wife for pursuit, and then add a female rival to complete the second triangle.

Vanbrugh was as diffident about his arrangement of events in *The Provok'd Wife* as he was about that in his first produced play: "I own," he wrote in "Vindication," "there is no mighty Plot in the whole matter" (I, 207). Instead, he attains his comic effects by rapid scene changes, wit combats, generous servings of farce, and a single scene (Act IV, scene 4) that outdoes even Congreve in the rich complexity of relationships displayed. A brief synopsis of *The Provok'd Wife* enables us to see more readily the episodic arrangement of events in which these effects are produced, the clarity of the relationships among the characters, and—most important—the resolutions of the two triangles, one a farcical success and the other an inconclusive and grim near failure.

In Act I, Sir John Brute's opening soliloquy announces the theme of the play—the misery of marriage. In spite of Lady Brute's efforts to please him, he insists on quarrelling; and she hints in her soliloquy that she might have her revenge by taking a lover. In the conversation that follows with her niece Bellinda, it becomes apparent that Lady Brute has a gallant in mind—Ned Constant. She swears, however, that she has given him no sign of her affections and that she will never be a coquette. In Scene 2, Lady Fancyfull, the vain and foolish neighbor of whom Bellinda and Lady Brute had talked, is introduced while at her toilette. Upon the receipt of an anonymous admiring letter, she is persuaded by her waiting woman Madamoiselle to go to the rendezvous it requests.

In Act II, at St. James's Park, Lady Fancyfull meets Heartfree, a noted woman-hater, who tells her that he will offer her his admiration if she will discard her affectation. But Lady Fancyfull, after defending her behavior as the effect of nice breeding, abruptly leaves. When Constant enters, complaining that his mistress, a married woman, is unresponsive, Heartfree tries without success to teach him to despise all women as vain. But, when Sir John Brute arrives, it becomes clear that it is Lady Brute whom Constant adores. Sir John's insults to his wife anger Constant, but Heartfree suggests that ill usage is the likeliest way to bring her to a gallant. In Scene 2, Lady Fancyfull, returned home, confesses that, in spite of Heartfree's ill treatment of her, she is favorably disposed toward him and considers writing to him.

In Act III, Sir John Brute is awaiting guests at home, and Bellinda and Lady Brute—who think Constant may be one of them—decide to wait too. As they do so, they offensively tease Sir John about his smoking and even hint at cuckoldry. At this point, the complications in the plot increase greatly when Sir John drives the women away at the very moment that Constant and Heartfree arrive; in so doing, Sir John not only shames his wife in public but also displays before Constant his mistreatment of her. When Sir John receives an invitation from some friends at a nearby tavern and asks the two visitors to wait for his return, they gladly agree; for Constant hopes to meet Lady Brute. In a moment, she and Bellinda enter; there is time only for the exchange of a few pleasantries before Lady Fancyfull arrives. She flirts again with Heartfree; but, finding him more interested in Bellinda, she soon leaves, followed by the company. When Lady Brute and Constant reenter, he confesses his love; and the two engage wittily in the classic courtly love debate about the nature and value of virtue. When she leaves and Heartfree enters, Constant is delirious with joy about the prospect of her returning his affection. In the meantime, Sir John is presented in Scene 2 at the Blue Posts Tavern as drunk; and the company roars coarse songs and plans an expedition into the streets. In Scene 3, Lady Brute and Bellinda, after some frank talk about man's passion and woman's vanity, consider accepting Constant and Heartfree, respectively, as lovers and plan to meet them again.

The play switches in Act IV to a street in Covent Garden where Sir John, having wounded somebody, now robs a tailor, puts on the parson's gown that he carries, challenges the watch, and is taken prisoner, while his cowardly companions flee. In Scene 2, the next morning, Heartfree discovers—to his dismay—that he is in love with Bellinda. Constant is delighted; and, after some badinage to revenge himself for Heartfree's earlier laughter at lovers, he encourages him to persevere. And so, when an anonymous letter arrives, inviting them to meet two women, Heartfree almost declines because of his love for Bellinda. On the same morning, Sir John Brute, still drunk and abusive (in Scene 3), is released by a justice of the peace because of his parson's gown—he goes in search of a whore.

Scene 4 brings all six of the principal characters together for the first time: Constant and Heartfree, dogged by a jealous Lady Fancyfull and her servant, arrive at Spring Garden where they discover two masked women (Lady Brute and Bellinda). But just as they begin to converse, Sir John Brute enters, mistakes the women for whores, and wishes to carry them off immediately. In a panic Lady Brute reveals herself to Constant and Bellinda to Heartfree; and, when the two young men offer the women their protection, Sir John leaves in a huff, still ignorant that he has been manhandling his own wife. The danger past, Heartfree confesses his love to Bellinda and even hints at matrimony, while Constant and Lady Brute renew their courtly love wit-combat. As Constant leads her toward a nearby arbor, the hiding place of the masked Lady Fancyfull and Madamoiselle, the two women rush out; Lady Brute is thrown into a frenzy of fear at being discovered; and the young men and their ladies flee. When Lady Fancyfull reenters, she promises her servant Madamoiselle that she will have revenge for losing Heartfree.

In Act V, Madamoiselle returns to Lady Fancyfull's to report that Constant and company are now at Lady Brute's; that Sir John is not at home; and that the only way to be revenged is to inform Sir John about his wife and Constant. In Scene 2, at the Brute's house, Lady Brute, Bellinda, Constant, and Heartfree are just sitting down to cards when Sir John rushes in, drunk and bloody. Constant and Heartfree hide in the closet; but Sir John, looking for some cold tea, breaks open the door and discovers the two gallants. Constant protests their innocence, but he also reminds Brute that he has a sword for satisfaction. After the two men leave him, Sir John mutters about his betrayal until he falls asleep; and Lady Brute and Bellinda agree upon a plan to allay Sir John's suspicion by claiming that the young men had come to the house because of Heartfree's love for Bellinda and had hidden themselves to prevent Sir John's wrong suspecting. Rasor, the valet, carries his master to bed but promises the audience to tell all to his own lover, Madamoiselle; and, in Scene 3, Lady Fancyfull urges Madamoiselle to ask Rasor to tell his master of the

near seduction in Spring Garden. When the valet arrives and re-
counts to Madamoiselle the events at Sir John's, she responds with
the Spring Garden story, but she acts out with Rasor the events that
transpired in order to arouse his passion. When Rasor agrees to tell
his master, Madamoiselle and Lady Fancyfull are left planning how
to prevent Heartfree's marriage.

In Scene 4, a letter from Lady Brute informs Constant of the plan
to pretend a marriage is afoot between Heartfree and Bellinda, and
Constant urges Heartfree to carry through and gain the woman he
loves. In Scene 5, the play moves rapidly to its denouement, when
the young men arrive at Sir John's to help convince him that the
closet affair was part of Heartfree's courtship of Bellinda. But
Heartfree and his inamorata quickly discover that their inclinations
are truly toward marriage and are not merely pretended. Sir John,
in spite of his continuing suspicions of his wife, announces himself
satisfied about her innocence in order to prevent Constant's challenge. A last minute scheme by Lady Fancyfull—to convince Bellinda that Heartfree is married and to warn him that Bellinda is
another man's mistress—is revealed by Rasor, who thus restores the
two lovers to each other and almost convinces Sir John that he is not
a cuckold. The play ends with Lady Fancyfull's flight and with the
promise of marriage between Heartfree and Bellinda.

The resolution of the Brute's love triangle in *The Provok'd Wife*,
as can be seen in this outline, is less than satisfactory dramatically as
well as maritally. The critics Mueschke and Fleisher, in fact, con-
tend that "the failure to bring the marital difficulties of the Brutes to
an issue on the stage involves not only a sacrifice of artistic effective-
ness, but also an evasion of any attempt to find a solution to the
problem of incompatibility. . . ."[1] Such an estimate of the play's
dramatic weakness, however, is an exaggeration; for Vanbrugh does
succeed in bringing a partial resolution to the Brute impasse. And
the charge that Vanbrugh evaded his responsibility in the matter of
marital incompatibility needs to be examined more closely.

In view of Sir John Brute's oft-reiterated statement that marriage
is his eternal aversion and also of his frequent exhibitions of physical
violence and his entire devotion to his bottle and his whore, there is
little likelihood that he will change by the end of the play; there is
virtual certainty that he will continue to abuse his wife and seek
pleasure away from home; therefore, a dramatic resolution based on
his reformation is impossible. Lady Brute, similarly, appears likely

to pursue the course she is now taking, one which will inevitably lead to adultery. For, as she confesses, she had married for money alone, had never loved her husband, had foolishly trusted that her charms could reform his beastly behavior, and has found her arguments for loyalty to her marriage vows more than matched by Constant's reasons for a pleasant revenge upon her husband for breaking his vows. In short, Sir John's aversion is fixed, his wife's patience is worn thin, a reconciliation is unlikely, and divorce with remarriage is impossible. Cuckoldry seems inevitable.

That Vanbrugh did not end his comedy with such a resolution is not so unsatisfactory, however, as may appear at first glance. Audiences are more moved by what they see on stage than by what they reason will occur after the play. The most dramatic event of the denouement, and what must affect them more immediately and more powerfully than the expectation of cuckolding, is Sir John's profound discomfiture in believing that his wife has given him horns. Everything he hears, feels, and smells is full of it; and his bitter retorts and asides are climaxed by his abject confession of cowardice: "And now, what shall I do with her——If I put my Horns in my Pocket, she'll grow Insolent——if I don't; that Goat there, that Stallion, is ready to whip me thro' the Guts.——The Debate then is reduc'd to this: Shall I die a Heroe? or live a Rascal?—— Why, Wiser Men than I, have long since concluded, that a living Dog is better than a dead Lion" (I, 178). Morever, Vanbrugh does not allow Brute to be convinced of his wife's innocence: his aside after Rasor's effort at vindicating her reputation is conclusive evidence that Sir John Brute is meant to receive punishment. "So that, after all," he says, " 'tis a Moot Point, whether I am a Cuckold or not" (I, 181).

Poetic justice is thus far served through Sir John. Lady Brute has been avenged, and she has escaped with her virtue intact, at least for the time being. Constant, to be sure, is frustrated in his designs; but he has more hopes at least than Chaucer's Aurelius. Furthermore, his situation cannot strike the audience as so desperate that he must be rescued as a part of the play's resolution. He is, after all, an accomplished rake who will "whore on" whatever Lady Brute does.

Apart from the incongruity of Lady Fancyfull's last minute insertion into the action and of Rasor's playing the puppet master in revealing her machinations, the ending of the subplot makes as neat

a package as one could wish, even to the rhymed couplet that warns
Heartfree and all husbands against Brutality:

HEART.   Then let's to Church:
         And if it be our Chance to disagree——
BELL.   Take heed—the surly Husband's Fate you see (I, 182).

II   The Characters of the Brute Triangle

In "Vindication," Captain Vanbrugh had at several points reiterated his belief that the plot should be a secondary consideration in
comic drama and that the characters are chiefly responsible for the
main business of the play—"to shew People what they shou'd do, by
representing them upon the Stage, doing what they shou'd not" (I,
206). Sir John Brute, of course, is the outstanding example in *The
Provok'd Wife* of a character who does what he should not do, whose
gross and violent action "gives the Spring," as Vanbrugh put it, "to
the rest of the Adventures" (I, 207). Like Sir Tunbelly Clumsey,
with whom Brute shares certain features, he is an original creation;
but unlike Sir Tunbelly, whose chief quality is his countrylike
coarseness, Sir John is the combination of a number of additional
qualities that had characterized previous Restoration stage types,
along with some unique Vanbrugh additions, that form the
marriage-hating, pleasure-loving, coward-bully that provided Betterton, Cibber, James Quin, David Garrick, and Charles Macklin
with the outstanding character role of the eighteenth century.

While the prime force in Brute's personality is his profound
hatred of marriage, the reasons for the depth of his misery are never
made clear. As a matter of fact, he appears to have every reason to
tolerate his wife, if not love her; for she possesses those qualities
that Vanbrugh's age expected in a woman. "My Lady," Brute confesses, "is a young Lady, a fine Lady, a Witty Lady, a virtuous
Lady,——and yet I hate her" (I, 115). If he had added *beautiful* and
patient, he would have completed the catalogue. It is not the woman, then, but the marital institution that Brute resents—the ines-
capable partnership that he has been contracted into that has driven
him to despair. "The Woman's well enough," he complains to Constant; "she has no Vice that I know of, but she's a Wife, and——
damn a Wife; If I were married to a Hogshead of Claret, Matrimony would make me hate it" (I, 130). From a wine-bibber like

Brute, this assertion is convincing evidence—if any more is needed—of his antipathy to the married state.

In this sentiment, Sir John Brute is in the mainstream of an old convention of Restoration comedy, one that Etherege had expressed some thirty years before in Sir Oliver Cockwood (*She Wou'd if She Cou'd*) in almost identical terms: "She is a Wife that no man need be asham'd of," Sir Oliver tells Courtall. But, "I would willingly give thee a pair of the best Coach-Horses in my Stable, so thou could'st but perswade her to love me less." And, "Well, a pox of this tying man and woman together, for better, for worse! upon my conscience it was but a Trick that the Clergy might have a feeling in the Cause."[2] As long as the marriage was founded, as with the Brutes, upon the man's lust and his lady's greed, and as long as divorce was—for all practical purposes—an impossibility, no additional reason for the misery of marriage need be sought than the certainty that one was trapped for life.

Sir John Brute's devotion to pleasure—to the Epicurean trinity of wine, women, and song—accords well with his character as a marriage-hater and places him beside Loveless and the Restoration rake stereotype as a Hobbesian libertine whose goal is to satisfy a succession of passions. The coarseness of his speech and conduct— his surly replies, his oaths, and his smoking, drunkenness, and carousing—mark him as a near relative to the ill-mannered squire who intruded upon the stage of many a seventeenth century comedy. These traits also contributed to the possibilities for farce in *The Provok'd Wife*, and they also enabled a succession of actors to hold the play on stage long after most of its rivals had sunk into oblivion. These traits also supplied the chief ingredients in those splendid quarrelling scenes which are among Vanbrugh's unique contributions to comedy. A near relation to the ill-mannered Clumsey on the Restoration boards is the bully-coward, the type that Congreve brought to perfection in Captain Bluffe in *The Old Batchelor* and in Petulant in *The Way of the World*. In two scenes Sir John exhibits as well the features that marked this type—the Covent Garden episode, in which he wounds a man in a street fight and attacks the constable and watchman, and the final scene in which he confesses himself a coward and pretends to believe in his wife's fidelity in order to avoid a duel.

This volatile combination of strongly marked qualities in the knight gave long life to the stage career of *The Provok'd Wife*, and the actors who were given the role—beginning with Thomas Betterton—considered it a prize. Their performances sparked a century long debate about the correct interpretation of the part—whether Sir John was to be a bestial coward or a loveable figure of fun—and his role became David Garrick's most successful stock in trade.[3] According to William Hazlitt, "This was Garrick's favourite part; and I have heard that his acting in the drunken scene . . . was irresistible."[4] The scenes in which Garrick excelled were two that Vanbrugh revised for one of the revivals of *The Provok'd Wife*—Brute's confrontation with the constable and later with the justice. In them Sir John's parson disguise is altered to that of a lady, and he delivers a sketch of a day in the life of a woman of quality that reminds us of Lord Foppington's "Round O" speech in *The Relapse*. The modifications may have been made as early as 1705 or as late as 1725,[5] but they seem to have given the comedy a new contract with fame and fortune, for the usual frontispiece illustration in the many eighteenth and nineteenth century collections containing the play invariably depicts Sir John Brute in female clothing.

Unlike her husband, who is clearly designed as Vanbrugh's bad example of a husband and a man, Lady Brute is another of the playwright's ambivalent creations; for she is at one and the same time a model to imitate and an example to avoid. Once again Vanbrugh deliberately shunned comic simplification in order to expose a problem that offers no easy solutions. As Vanbrugh indicated in "Vindication," the lady's provocation comes from a brute rather than a more rational being like Loveless; consequently it could not be expected to affect her decisions as strongly:

The Lady therefore that gives her self a Loose upon it, cou'd not naturally be represented the best of her Sex. Virtuous (upon some ground or other) there was a Necessity of making her; but it appears by a Strain of Levity that runs through her Discourse, she ow'd it more to Form, or Apprehension, or at best to some few Notions of Gratitude to her Husband, for taking her with an Inferior Fortune, than to any Principle of Religion, or an extraordinary Modesty. 'Twas therefore not extremely to be wondred at, that when her Husband made her House uneasy to her at home, she shou'd be prevail'd with to accept of some Diversions abroad (I, 212).

The "strain of levity" that runs through Lady Brute's speeches relating to virtue is only part of the evidence that her fidelity is not strongly rooted, for the lines she delivers in anger, as well as her conduct in Spring Garden, reveal how near she has come to accepting a lover. Her irate soliloquy in the first scene, for example, following Sir John's cross-grained quibbling, ends with her explosive "Virtue's its own reward, Virtue's this, Virtue's that——Virtue's an Ass, and a Gallant's worth forty on't" (I, 117). And her near seduction by Constant promises to have been successful had it not been for Lady Fancyfull's interruption.

The scenes between Bellinda and Lady Brute, however, seem to be intended as the stronger evidence of her not overvirtuous nature. In the first of these, following immediately upon her soliloquy, she tells her niece that she has almost been provoked into cuckolding her husband, that Constant's attentions are an ever-present temptation, and that her own hunger for affection is leading her toward what her soul scarcely dares to confess. Within this context, the second scene should be read; for there the flippancy of her exchanges with Bellinda about Constant might otherwise suggest past performance as much as present inclination or wishful thinking:

LADY BRUTE. He has besieg'd me these two Years to no Purpose.

BELL. And if he besieg'd you two Years more, he'd be well enough paid, so he had the plundering of you at last.

LADY BRUTE. That may be; but I'm afraid the Town won't be able to hold out much longer; for to confess the Truth to you, *Bellinda*, the Garrison begins to grow mutinous.

BELL. Then the sooner you capitulate, the better.

LADY BRUTE. Yet methinks I wou'd fain stay a little longer, to see you fix'd too, that we might start together, and see who cou'd love longest. What think you, if *Heartfree* shou'd have a Month's Mind to you?

. . . . .

BELL. What shou'd I do with him, he has no Fortune: I can't marry him; and sure you wou'd not have me commit Fornication.

LADY BRUTE. Why if you did, Child, 'twou'd be but a good friendly part; if 'twere only to keep me in Countenance whilst I commit——You know what (I, 150–51).

Parallel to these exchanges between the two ladies—and surely Vanbrugh's wit debates between women are the finest in Restoration comedy—are the scenes in which Lady Brute and Constant confront each other in the classic Restoration love-combat. Here, however, her position is abruptly reversed, appropriately enough; for instead of arguing her way toward adultery, she counters each of

Constant's sallies in favor of an affair with a reply that displays her intellect without diminishing her good nature. The love he offers is an offense, she tells him in their first exchange, "a great one, where it wou'd rob a Woman of all she ought to be ador'd for; her Virtue" (I, 143). When he promises that her love would make him her everlasting debtor, she returns with "When Debtors once have borrow'd all we have to lend, they are very apt to grow very shy of their Creditor's Company" (I, 144).

This argument is the one to which she returns in their second exchange (Act IV, scene 4), for it is painfully clear to her that her present situation is the result of Sir John's loss of interest after he had possessed her. "Your Sufferings eas'd, your Flame wou'd soon abate," she tells Constant, "And that I wou'd preserve, not quench it, Sir."

> CONST. Wou'd you preserve it, nourish it with favours; for that's the Food, it naturally requires.
> LADY BRUTE. Yet on that Natural Food, 'twou'd surfeit soon, shou'd I resolve to grant all that you wou'd ask (I, 164).

So ends the debate, for all of their exchanges return to the same unresolvable issue. Action is Constant's answer, and it almost carries the day.

What seems to lie behind Lady Brute's resistance to Constant's solicitations, more than fear or gratitude or habit as Vanbrugh had suggested in "Vindication," is her certain knowledge that she has brought her present misery upon herself. As she says of her husband in her soliloquy, "The Devil's in the Fellow I think——I was told before I married him, that thus 'twou'd be; But I thought I had Charms enough to govern him; and that where there was an Estate, a Woman must needs be happy; so my Vanity has deceiv'd me, and my Ambition has made me uneasie. . . . I never lov'd him . . . " (I, 116). For an intelligent woman, such a confession of failure must be especially painful; for, besides absolving Sir John of much of the responsibility for the misery of their marriage and placing it on herself, her admission is a reminder that the decision she is now contemplating may also be an error. Her originality as a dramatic character, then, lies in the fact that she is conscious of her own responsibility for her unhappiness; and she knows not only that what she is contemplating is sinful, but, more important, that the cuckolding of her husband would as much confess her bad judgment as punish his bad conduct. Like Lady Brute, Constant is left at the end of *The Provok'd Wife* with neither punishment nor reward. Although he is given the wit, the persistence, and the good looks of his brother Restoration rakes, and although he shares with them the requisite cynical attitude toward women, he neither wins his lady during the course of the comedy nor is promised her at its final curtain. He "gives himself a great deal of trouble," said Vanbrugh in "Vindication," "for a thing that is not worth his Pains" (I, 208). In so doing, Constant illustrates once again Vanbrugh's argument that comedy teaches by acting on stage what people should not do.

In so arguing, Vanbrugh signalled his intent to create a gentleman wit more closely allied to Worthy than to Horner, one who could break the stage stereotype of the heartless cynic, one who could demonstrate a capacity for sincere love, and one who willingly considers seriously its implications. Constant has persisted for two years in the adoration of his lady; is so overwhelmed at the thought of speaking with her that he almost faints; and, after his first exchange of words with her, is so ecstatic that he is ready to run mad. He is, in short, "a whining Lover" (as Heartfree called him), "the damn'dst Companion upon Earth" (I, 131), an exponent of that courtly love principle according to which woman is considered to be a goddess, the object of slavish adoration by her admirers.[6] This principle, to be sure, was laughed at in prose and poetry throughout and after the seventeenth century; for example, it was treated with wry bitterness by John Donne in "The Funeral," and with light-hearted amusement by Pope in "The Rape of the Lock." Restoration comedy, in turn, mocked the Lady Cockwoods, the Fidgets, and the Wishforts for the falsity of their *précieuse* decorum; and Lady Fancyfull is Vanbrugh's own satire on the affectation, the assumption of superlative beauty and moral superiority, and the emphasis on honor that such godlike females were supposed to display.

Although Vanbrugh had used "whining" in a pejorative sense, he did not intend that Constant should be considered entirely ridiculous, nor that the possibility of a perfect love and a perfect marriage should be quite ruled out. Indeed, Constant's reply to Sir John Brute is meant sincerely: "You are a true *Englishman;* Don't know your own Happiness: if I were married to such a Woman, I would not be from her a Night for all the Wine in *France*" (I, 129). Even his

tirade against the "Chains of Wedlock" (I, 144) recognizes the possibility of a happy union:

LADY BRUTE. Have you no exceptions to this General Rule?
CONST. Yes: I would (after all) be an exception to it my self, if you were
free, in Power and Will to make me so.

And his words to Heartfree at the end of Act V, scene 4, though
they reject marriage in general, also admit the possibility of the
ideal exception: "For tho' Marriage be a Lottery in which there are a
wondrous many Blanks; yet there is one inestimable Lot, in which
the only Heaven on Earth is written. Wou'd your kind Fate but
guide your hand to that, tho' I were wrapt in all that Luxury itself
could cloath me with, I still shou'd envy you" (I, 176).

Nevertheless, unlike Loveless and Worthy in *The Relapse*, Constant retains the verve and dash of a comedy of manners rake. The
constancy of his adoration, it should be remembered, has but one
end, adultery. For him, a married woman's virtue is no more than
"That Phantome of Honour, which men in every Age have so con-
temn'd, they have thrown it amongst the Women to scrabble for" (I,
143). He can see the absurdity of his own devotion, and he can laugh
at Heartfree when the tables are turned and his friend is in love.
And, if we read accurately Heartfree's allusions to his friend's
amours, he upholds the stage rake's reputation for lasciviousness. In
short, as Vanbrugh put it, "I have laid open his Vices as well as his
Virtues: 'Tis the Business of the Audience to observe where his
Flaws lessen his Value; and by considering the Deformity of his
Blemishes, become sensible how much a Finer Thing he wou'd be
without 'em" (I, 206–07).

III   *Heartfree, Bellinda, and Lady Fancyfull*

There is little enough to distinguish Heartfree from Constant in
The Provok'd Wife; they are given equal amounts of wit and like
amounts of passion; each has a series of speeches in which he rails
against love and marriage; and each is allowed about the same
number of lines in which to express his love for his lady. Vanbrugh
even balances a scene in Heartfree's lodgings against one in Constant's; and in two scenes each is given in turn a center stage wit-
combat with his mistress. More important, however, is the fact that

both are romantics who believe, as Heartfree says, that "to be capable of loving one . . . is better than to possess a Thousand" (I, 176). Not only do they confess to one another that they love, but, to the eternal shame of all self-respecting rakes, they also agree that perfect marriage is a possibility—a remote one perhaps—but still a possibility. Even their vices are balanced—Constant is more notably the whore-master, and Heartfree is overly fond of the bottle.

But there are differences enough between the two to make each his own man, and Heartfree's situation and inclinations are such as to make him the nearest thing to a hero in the comedy. We meet him first as a woman-hater, to be sure, but his aversion is neither a snarling one like Sir John Brute's nor a hypocritical one like his brother Heartwell's in Congreve's *The Old Batchelor* (1693). Furthermore, it is clear from his extravagant praise for Lady Fancyfull that he could love if the woman were free from affectation;[7] and it is plain from the following scene with Constant that he has a very rational fear of being "used like a dog" (a phrase he employs twice) by the woman to whom he might give his heart.

With his misogyny thus qualified, Heartfree rapidly begins to gain sympathy with the audience, not only for his wit—which is considerable—but because he is a fortuneless younger brother and because his courtship is respectable since it is directed toward Bellinda, an unmarried woman whose possession of the one quality he seeks is evidence of his good judgment. He also endears himself by exhibiting in Act IV, scene 2, all the symptoms of lovesickness (including an amusing Freudian slip that alerts Constant to his changed state) by refusing at first to go with Constant to meet the Spring Garden women, whom he believes to be whores, and then, when he does meet them, by turning them over with great relief to Sir John Brute.

As to Heartfree's wit, nearly all of it at the expense of women, Vanbrugh seems to have taken special pains with what he called in "Vindication" his hero's "extravagant Railing at Womankind," particularly his Act II speech on curing love. The first half of Heartfree's discourse anticipates Addison's dissection of a coquette's heart in the *Spectator* (no. 281, January 22, 1712): "I always consider a Woman [says Heartfree, I, 128] turn'd inside out. Her Heart well examin'd, I find there Pride, Vanity, Covetousness, Indiscretion, but above all things, Malice; . . ." The second, and more powerful, half of his discourse may have influenced Swift's *A Tale of a Tub:*

Then for her Outside, I consider it merely as an Outside; She has a thin
Tiffany Covering over just such Stuff as you and I are made on.
As for her Motion, her Mien, her Airs, and all those Tricks, I know they
affect you mightily. If you should see your Mistriss at a Coronation, drag-
ging her Peacock's Train, with all her state and insolence about her, 'twoud
strike you with all the awful thoughts that Heav'n it self could pretend to
from you; whereas I turn the whole matter into a Jest, and suppose her
strutting in the self-same stately manner, with nothing on her but her Stays
and her under scanty quilted Petticoat.

Here, says Augustine Birrell, who much admires Vanbrugh as a man
of ideas, "appears the Philosophy of Clothes (thus forestalling Swift),
and also an early conception of Carlyle's stupendous image of a
naked House of Lords."[8]

When one recalls that Vanbrugh himself remained unmarried
until his fifty-fifth year, it is not difficult to image his subscribing, in
general at least, to Heartfree's wittily stated principles. At any rate,
some twenty-two years after the *The Provok'd Wife* appeared, Vanbrugh could recall Heartfree's apprehensive aside as he contemplates his impending marriage to Bellinda: "So, now, I am in for
Hob's Voyage; a great Leap in the Dark" (I, 177). Sir John's own
marriage had already occurred, to be sure, but he still had his
doubts when on July 1, 1719, he wrote to publisher Jacob Tonson,
then in Paris: "Here has been so great a Slaughter of your old
Friends since you went, I wish those who are left may have share
enough in your Affections, to encline you to think of England with
any pleasure. I don't know whether you'll reckon me amongst the
first or the last, since I have taken *this great Leap in the Dark* [italics
added], Marriage. . . . I am confirmed (as far as Six months practice
goes) my Old Opinion was right; That whatever there was of good or
bad in Marriage; it was fitter to end Our Life with, than begin it" (I,
111).

The woman with whom Heartfree agrees to make the dark exper-
iment in *The Provok'd Wife* is intended by Captain Vanbrugh as a
perfect match for his hero. Bellinda has frankness enough to satisfy
Heartfree's aversion to affectation, sufficient wit to match his verbal
cleverness, and more than enough innocence to accord with his
reluctance to fall in love and with his relative inexperience with sex.
Young and virginal though she may be, however, Bellinda is no
naive Hoyden or Prue in search of amours. She knows that woman's
charms depend upon her modesty and that fornication without mar-

riage is a poor last resort for a woman of intelligence. Her scheme to allay Sir John's suspicions by a real or pretended marriage to Heartfree, thus killing two birds with one stone, is evidence of her ingenuity; and her readiness to accept "the Man I love, and a Middle State of Life" (I, 169) reveals a degree of good judgment that even Daniel Defoe might have approved.

The rare combination in Bellinda, however, of clever speech and honest conduct serves to adorn her virtuous nature to perfection. She can create the aphoristic antitheses so admired by the pit, as she does in her reply to Heartfree's proposal of marriage (a bon mot reminiscent of Berinthia's "Babies" speech): "Well, you Men are unaccountable things, mad till you have your Mistresses; and then stark mad till you are rid of 'em again" (I, 162). And, to Heartfree's urging, "Do but try me," she responds: "That's the surest way indeed, to know, but not the safest" (I, 162). At the same time, she has no pretensions to being thought a lady wit; and she wins her beau through frank speech and unaffected manners. In fact, it is her liking for plain talk that brings Heartfree to express his love for her:

BELL. Now has my Vanity a devilish Itch, to know in what my Merit consists.

HEART. In your Humility, Madam, that keeps you ignorant it consists at all.

. . .

HEART. Some Women love to be abus'd: Is that it you wou'd be at?

BELL. No, not that neither: But I'd have Men talk plainly what's fit for Women to hear; without putting 'em either to a real or an affected Blush.

HEART. Why then, in as plain Terms as I can find to express my self, I cou'd love you even to—Matrimony it self a-most I-gad (I, 162).

Lady Fancyfull, Bellinda's rival for Heartfree's attention, is, of course, the very antithesis of plain speaking and unaffected acting. That she is a serious rival is apparent from Heartfree's earnest effort to reform her and from his extravagant praise of her natural graces, "Beauty to a Miracle, a Shape without a fault, Wit enough to make 'em relish . . ." (I, 126). She lacks, however, any capacity to change and persists to the end as the other considerable figure of fun in *The Provok'd Wife*. In this role, Lady Fancyfull is very much in the stage tradition of the female fop, the *précieuse* of the type of Melantha in Dryden's *Marriage à la Mode* (1672), after whom she is very likely modelled. Melantha, too, like Fancyfull, affects a passion for everything French, bestows gifts upon her maid depending upon how extravagantly she is praised, and is constantly making her entrances and exits on the run. The single quality these ladies share is a notion of their beauty, wit, and virtue so extravagant that they think themselves the cynosure of all neighboring eyes, male or female. "Lard," says Lady Fancyfull, with Lord Foppington's pronunciation as well as his arrogance, "why was I form'd to make the whole Creation uneasy?" (I, 122). She can argue the rightness of her conduct against the whole world, and she can scarcely value any man's attentions since they are "so infinitely my due." Convinced thus of her infallibility as well as of her beauty, Lady Fancyfull is quick to display envy and malice where she detects a rival—and she is equally quick to exhibit evidence of rare qualities in her temperament and talent. Thus she is eager to tell her little court of her dream that, "by an unanimous Vote, I was chosen Queen of [the moon]," and "all my Subjects fell in Love with me" (I, 132). The image is ludicrous enough, but an audience is reminded that, besides its associations with Diana, the moon has some close connections with lunacy. Similarly, she boasts of singing in the park late one night and of receiving the next morning three poems and six love letters. But, shades of Samuel Johnson!, the song she sang was "Chevy Chase"; and few street ballads are longer, bloodier, or duller than it. Her decision to seek revenge is similarly ludicrous, for it is made without thought and is executed in the crudest fashion.

"Lady *Fanciful*," said Vanbrugh in "Vindication," "is ridicul'd for her Vanity and her Affectation" (I, 208). In adding to the denouement of the comedy a set of farcical complications, he made of her ultimately a comic rather than a malicious figure; and, by doing so, he avoided the dark and melodramatic extremes in characters like Congreve's Lady Touchwood and Mrs. Marwood.

The only two remaining characters of any importance in *The Provok'd Wife* are the servants Rasor and Madamoiselle, both stereotypes, both contributing in important ways to the comic success of the play. Madamoiselle is a typical "*Suivante* of her Countrey," said Vanbrugh in "Vindication"; and Rasor represents the familiar type of the clever English servant. Madamoiselle's role is primarily that of confidante to the Frenchified Lady Fancyfull, and her lines are almost entirely in the language of her native country—a fact that seemingly confirms the Bastille origin of the comedy. The two servants match the two love triangles in a third geometric figure, a quadrangle, in which their fondness for each other is counterbalanced by loyalty to their respective employers. Thus Madamoiselle is quick to exploit Rasor for her mistress's advantage, and Rasor is equally ready to expose the lady and her maid for the sake of the Brute family. The two servants together, however, provide one of the finest—but also the bawdiest—comic vignettes in the play when they act out the Spring Garden meeting of Constant and Lady Brute. William Hazlitt, who did much to arrest the decline of Vanbrugh's reputation in the nineteenth century, considered the scene inimitable, a superb example of his author's ability to create dramatic tours de force of this kind: "Nothing [he wrote] was ever more happily conceived, or done to more absolute perfection."[9]

IV   *Interpreting the Puppet Show*

In "A Short Vindication of *The Relapse* and *The Provok'd Wife*," Vanbrugh had professed to believe that by nature comedy had a moral force, that the display of vice or folly on stage was itself a corrective, and hence the audience needed no special insights to recognize what action was meant to be emulated and what to be avoided. "Nor is there any necessity," he wrote, "a Philosopher shou'd stand by, like an Interpreter at a Poppet-show, to explain the Moral to the Audience: The Mystery is seldom so deep, but the Pit and Boxes can dive into it" (I, 206). He was not alone, of course, in the belief that to show vice and folly was to discourage them. Virtually all the dramatists and critics who responded to Collier took the same tack. One of the replies, by Cibber, came in a brief dialogue in Act V of *The Careless Husband* (1704) that not only reiterates Vanbrugh's thesis but also suggests the heart of the problem:

LORD MORELOVE. Plays now indeed one need not be so much afraid of, for since the late short-sighted View of 'em, Vice may go on and prosper, the Stage dares hardly shew a Vicious Person speaking like himself, for fear of being call'd Prophane for exposing him.

LADY EASY. 'Tis Hard indeed, when People won't Distinguish between what's Meant for Contempt, and what for Example.[10]

The distinction of which Lady Easy speaks is not all that simple, of course, in Vanbrugh's plays generally or in *The Provok'd Wife*. This second original comedy was like the first in mixing moral and immoral characters and actions in the same dramatic work. Whether, for instance, Constant or Bellinda or Lady Brute are contemptible or exemplary is not so simple a decision that a philosopher's advice isn't welcome.

The attack by Collier, calling Vanbrugh to task for a variety of offenses, had been grounded in the premise that the playwright was being deliberately immoral throughout the play, that "when Vice is varnish'd over with Pleasure, and comes in the Shape of Conveni-ence, the case grows somewhat dangerous; for then the Fancy may be gain'd, and the Guards corrupted, and Reason suborn'd against it self."[11] Collier's view is a rather different interpretation from Van-brugh's of the showing of vice and folly upon the stage. But Collier's pistol misfired in his examples, for Constant is not rewarded for his pains in pursuing Lady Brute; Bellinda—condemned for confessing that she could accept a lover—is brought to a promising marriage; and Lady Brute may talk about a gallant but doesn't take one.

Instead, the reforming divine might have charged the playwright where a defense could not so easily be made if he had attacked the Spring Garden scene and its reenactment by the two servants. The near seduction of Lady Brute, to be sure, can be performed so that it is only slightly suggestive, but her words indicate a willingness that comes close to Berinthia's. The reenactment by Rasor and Madamoiselle is far more explicit; for, in spite of the conservative stage directions—"*Rasor* struggles with her, as if he would throw her down" (I, 173)—Madamoiselle's words describe a performance of the sex act on stage:

> Den he grow bold.
> She grow weak.
> He tro her down.
> Il tombe dessu, [He falls on top]
> Le Diable assist, [The Devil helps]
> Il emport tout: [He wins out] (I, 173)

The French servant is following the instructions of her mistress, to be sure, not to refuse Rasor "a few little reasonable Liberties, to put him into humour" (I, 171); but, since her enthusiasm goes beyond mere obedience, it reflects her role in the play as a rep-resentative of the philosophy of libertinism, the belief that the end of life should be pleasure and that every effort should be made to achieve it.[12] Vanbrugh has been careful not only to make her func-

tion effectively in the plot by giving her the speeches that encourage
Lady Fancyfull to rendezvous with her anonymous admirer but also
to make her a consistent spokesman for the pursuit of pleasure as a
way of live. "If you never Love, you never be Happy" (I, 122), she
tells her mistress; and she encourages her to continue to add lovers
to her following. She is eager to see Lady Fancyfull involved in an
affair, even if her reputation must suffer. "Why sure you wou'd not
sacrifice your Honor to your Pleasure?" exclaims Lady Fancyfull.
"Quand quelque chose m'incommode moy—je m'en defais, Vite,"
replies Madamoiselle: "When something inconveniences me, I
overcome it, quickly" (I, 123). And, when Lady Fancyfull argues
that reason should correct natural impulses, Madamoiselle ends
their debate with "My nature make me merry, my reason make me
mad" (I, 124).

By putting libertine principles in the mouth of a French servant,
however, Vanbrugh seems to have intended them to be ridiculed.
That intent was, at least, the burden of his reply to Collier. But it is
a moot point whether all parts of the audience would agree that
Madamoiselle's words and actions are a discouragement to vice, or
(for that matter) that Lady Brute's Spring Garden adventure is a
discouragement to virtue. As Vanbrugh did in *The Relapse,* he gives
us a play with actions that are both moral and immoral, a play that
presents good and evil so inextricably intertwined that even
philosophers must disagree in distinguishing which is which. What
the ladies of the boxes applaud, the gentlemen of the pit are likely to
hiss. The extremes in conduct that are clearly ridiculed—the gross
and cowardly behavior of Sir John Brute and the vanity and affectation of Lady Fancyfull—are the easiest part of the problem. The
hardest questions go into a realm of moral and ethical complexity far
beyond the simple answers that comedy ordinarily provides.

Most important among these questions is what conduct by Lady
Brute is intended for our imitation and what for our contempt. Is the
audience to applaud the encouragement Vanbrugh's heroine gives
her gallant or to hiss the threat to her marriage vows? Vanbrugh's
answer appears to be an uncomic compromise: Lady Brute is
punished for her flirtation with Constant by her deep embarrassment in the Spring Garden and in the Cold Tea episodes. And the
threat to her marital fidelity is deferred at least, and perhaps
averted, by that embarrassment as well as by Bellinda's marriage
and hence (presumably) the end of flirtatious escapades by the two

women. At the same time, Lady Brute has a limited revenge upon her husband, as has been pointed out earlier, for his gross misconduct. It is *limited* in that she has not taken the final step, but it is *revenge* in that her husband is convinced that she has broken her marriage vow.

The still larger question in the play is what can be done, practically speaking, about an impossible marriage? Vanbrugh's answer is that nothing can be done; no compromise is possible for a woman like Lady Brute. In their analysis of the dramatic ending of *The Provok'd Wife*, Mueschke and Fleisher conclude that Vanbrugh should have brought the comedy to some sort of resolution, either exploding the notion of the double standard by allowing his heroine to commit adultery, or permitting her to gain some measure of independence from her boorish husband by means of divorce or separation.[13] But divorce, as Gellert Alleman has since shown, was in practical terms an impossibility since the only grounds— adultery—meant scandal and since remarriage in any case was an impossibility.[14] Separation, in like manner, was almost as unthinkable, for in no age before our own has it been possible for a woman to live alone without blackening her reputation.

Finally, Vanbrugh could not accept cuckoldry as a solution for Lady Brute: if entered into as revenge, it would have been, as I have already observed, a humiliating confession that her charms had failed to reform Sir John, as well as a potential repetition of her earlier mistake of thinking a man's lust was love. If Vanbrugh had committed her to adultery, merely or primarily out of passion, he would have been denying what he believed to be woman's most basic characteristic—expressed in Constant's words—"Women are not naturally lewd." *The Provok'd Wife* is not, in short, The Intelligent Woman's Guide to Adultery. "Wives do Cuckold their Husbands," said Vanbrugh; but Lady Brute considers herself to be a woman of understanding (as evidenced in her first conversation with Constant) with other options still at her disposal; and she believes women to be wiser than men and, through that wisdom and their sexual appeal, to be the governors of the world. What those other options may be must elude reasonable speculation, but Sir John's gross misbehavior has been of such recent date—as she says in her soliloquy—that we cannot imagine that her reason has brought her so soon to the conclusion that there is no hope for some sort of reconciliation.

The more forceful impression made by the play, however, is that the Brute marriage is a failure and that both partners are likely to continue in unhappiness. The inevitable conclusion must be, therefore, that, since marriage is an unbreakable contract, it may become a perpetual bondage. If one must marry, Vanbrugh tells his audience, he must marry with caution: one should marry for love and not for lust or money; better yet, one should marry late if he would take no chance on prolonging potential agony. If we can trust Lady Mary Wortley Montagu's letter of November 1713, and if we recall Vanbrugh's letter to Tonson,[15] it is clear that the playwright took both pieces of advice in marrying Henrietta Yarburgh on the threshold of his old age.

CHAPTER 5

Translated from the French

A FTER the premiere of *The Provok'd Wife* in April 1697, Vanbrugh never again returned to the stage with an original play.
Beginning with *Aesop* in December 1696, all but one of his produced comedies were translations from the varied body of contemporaneous French drama. Although many of these productions have
merits of one kind or another—*Aesop* is praised, for example, for its
masterly rendition of the aphorisms of Boursault; *The Confederacy*,
for the true to life vigor of its low characters—they are, after all,
close adaptations of the original plots; and, for that reason alone,
they have attracted little critical attention.

Furthermore, only *The Confederacy*, *Aesop*, and *The Country
House* had any kind of success during the poet's lifetime; and none
of the plays continued long in the theaters later in the century. The
single exception to the rule is Vanbrugh's rendition of Fletcher's
The Pilgrim, the only adaptation that did not come from the French,
which took the stage seventy-one times in Vanbrugh's lifetime, and
outplayed *The Relapse* and *The Provok'd Wife* in recorded productions. For these reasons, then, because the plots are borrowed and
because the comedies in general were not popular and added little
to Vanbrugh's reputation, most of them require only a cursory
treatment in any work about his contributions to comic drama.

The six adaptations that Vanbrugh prepared for the stage have
little in common as regards plot, characters, and theme. Their selection for translation or alteration indicates, of course, that the English
playwright was familiar with a considerable body of current French
dramatic literature and that his mastery of the language was such
that he was at home in rendering idiomatic French into its English
equivalent. His linguistic and dramatic skill, in addition, accorded
well with current taste; for, shortly after Betterton's revolt in 1695,

116

the two competing playhouses began to draw upon the wealth of lively French farces that Molière and his successors had been bringing to the stages of Paris and provincial France.

But Vanbrugh seems to have selected each of his plays for specific qualities and to achieve a variety of ends. *Aesop*, taken from Boursault and produced in December 1696, seems to have been chosen to suit the comic talents of the Drury Lane troupe, particularly those of Cibber, Doggett, Penkethman, and Mrs. Verbruggen. The translation of Dancourt's *The Country House* (performed January 1698) was very likely made for the same reason. The one alteration from the English, Fletcher's *The Pilgrim* (April 1700), was selected, as has been noted, as a representative of great English comedy in honor of England's greatest contemporaneous tragic poet, John Dryden. What brought Vanbrugh to translate Lesage's *Le Traître Puni* for the Drury Lane actors is less clear; his version, *The False Friend* (produced February 1702), is so full of tragic events—a dying father, an attempted rape, a murder plot, and a violent death—that it deserves some other name than comedy. It is, of course, a fine actor's vehicle; but it is otherwise melodramatic in effect and improbable in plot. The last two of Vanbrugh's adaptations were minor comic masterpieces in the original; hence, they appeared to be just the fare to give the new Queen's Theatre the stage successes it so desperately needed. Dancourt's best play, *Les Bourgeoises à la Mode,* opened in October 1705 as *The Confederacy;* and Molière's lively intrigue comedy, *Le Dépit Amoureux,* took the stage the following December as *The Mistake.*

In all of these adaptations, Vanbrugh may be said to have made two contributions: his gift for choosing vivid words and colorful English expressions is apparent throughout; and, by adding scenes and cutting passages of dialogue, he speeds the movement and increases the farcical quality of each play. Only two of his selections from French drama, however, are sufficiently altered to be more than translations—*The Confederacy,* with its new opening and added scenes, and *Aesop,* with its shifting of scenes and its much altered ending. Vanbrugh's modifications in the remaining four plays—the creation of a new character, an occasional softening or enlivening of language, the turning of poetry into prose, and the various other changes that make each work a more English play—are noted in our discussion.

I   Aesop I and II

The least plotted of the adaptations, *Aesop*, exhibits both Vanbrugh's strengths and weaknesses. He believed that story is less
important than characterization, and he had proved that tenet in
The Relapse and *The Provok'd Wife*. In Édme Boursault's *Les Fables
d'Ésope*, Vanbrugh found an episodic plot so intractable that no
tinkering could improve it.[1] Although he altered the fifth act by
omitting scenes unrelated to the main plot and by changing the
resolution so that the father is discomfitted rather than won over to
his daughter's new marriage, he added little more than empty bustle to an already lost dramatic cause. The prologue, as a matter of
fact, attempted to avert criticism of the weak story line by announcing in advance, "No Hero, no Romance, no Plot, no Show,/ No
Rape, no Bawdy, no Intrigue, no Beau" (II, 11). Instead, Vanbrugh
succeeded best in making the characters more lively and in creating
a minor dramatic masterpiece *à la* Sir Tunbelly Clumsey in the
person of Sir Polidorus Hogstye.

Aesop consists essentially of two pieces of material: the story of
Learchus's unsuccessful effort to marry his daughter to Aesop forms
the thinnest of plots; and a series of exchanges between Aesop and
persons who come to ask his advice is inserted at frequent intervals.
The main story line is hung upon Learchus's design to preserve his
position as governor of Syzicus by marrying Euphronia to the
influential but ugly philosopher Aesop. Euphronia, of course, loves
elsewhere, a young man named Oronces; and she and her nurse
Doris attempt to gain Aesop's aid in bringing the two young people
together. At Learchus's insistance, Aesop reluctantly agrees to
marry Euphronia, but only if she will consent. Both Euphronia and
Oronces appear to fail in their appeals to Aesop for aid, and Doris's
plots come to nothing. Just as the wedding ceremony concludes,
however, Aesop joins the hands of the two young lovers; and the
priest pronounces them one. To Learchus, Aesop promises punishment for his cruelty: "I shall take Care this City may be sway'd/ By
more Humanity than dwells in you" (II, 61).

Introduced at irregular intervals among the pieces of this episodic
action are various persons who come to ask Aesop's advice. His
response is usually delivered in the form of a rhymed fable: two
tradesmen are told the story of the rebellious hands and feet in
order to teach them the need for cooperation among the social

classes; a country bumpkin who would go to court is treated to the
fable of the city mouse and his country cousin. A lewd mother is
warned that her daughter will follow her example; an envious widow
is cautioned with the tale of the toad who tried to swell to the size of
an ox; Sir Polidorus Hogstye is ridiculed for his bad treatment of his
wife and tenants; and Mr. and Mrs. Fruitful are chastized for bringing up children who are no credit to God or country.

Outstanding among the characters whom Vanbrugh added to
Boursault's catalogue of fools is Sir Polidorus Hogstye, a drunken
country gentleman who has all the rustic crudeness of Sir Tunbelly
Clumsey and who has the wife-hating irascibility of Sir John Brute.
Hogstye cheats on his taxes, grinds down his tenants, and treats his
wife "all Day with ill Nature and Tobacco; and all Night with Snor-
ing, and a dirty Shirt." But his appearance is brief, no more than a
stage caricature; and, though it afforded an amusing interlude, it
could not save the play—nor could the addition of the Fruitfuls or
even the farcical introduction in the last scene of an Aesop in fop's
clothing—the part that so delighted Cibber.

Part two of *Aesop*, added to the comedy some three months after
its opening at Drury Lane, consisted of three interviews between
Aesop and his visitors. The first of the scenes in *Aesop II* is clearly
modelled on one of those discarded when Vanbrugh translated
Aesop I.[2] Its chief purpose was to laugh the two theaters back into a
union by comparing the rebellious Betterton and company to a set of
mutinous crewmen who, on the slightest pretext, have thrown off
the authority of their captain. The fable that Aesop offers in order to
bring them back, the story of a pack of starving beagles, served its
purpose in the play, but not in real life. The union was not to be
accomplished until 1708 and the establishment of opera at Queen's.

The remaining scenes in *Aesop II* are original with Vanbrugh. The
second one returns to the theme that Boursault had pursued in the
original *Les Fables d'Ésope*, and that Vanbrugh had employed in Sir
Polidorus Hogstye—the bumpkin who complains of the government
or who would go to court to correct it. A country senator approaches
Aesop with a scheme to improve the government by replacing the
chief ministers with his own relatives. But, when Aesop asks him to
employ the displaced courtiers as bailiff and huntsman on his estate,
the senator sees at a glance how ill-equipped they would be for
those tasks; hence, he realizes how badly prepared his relatives are
for court posts. The last scene swings to the opposite extreme by

bringing on stage "a Young Gay Airy Beau" of the type of Lord Foppington; but he is far more foolish, depraved, and diseased. Despite the moral ugliness in the character that he reveals to Aesop, however, the beau ends the episode with a fable to his own advantage: he proves that ladies always prefer the airs of the beau to the solid qualities of other men.

II   The Country House

Only slightly more complicated in plot is the next piece that Vanbrugh chose to translate from the French, Florent Dancourt's *La Maison de Campagne* (1688). The country atmosphere that prevails in the English revision has something in it of the Tunbelly Clumsey scenes in *The Relapse* and the Hogstye episode in *Aesop*. There is the same high speed rough and tumble, the visual jokes, the oaths, the coarseness, the abrasive juxtapositioning of crude and refined characters. What Vanbrugh finds at length in the French original is what had formed only an episode in two of his earlier works.

The story of *The Country House* is that of a wealthy but frugal lawyer whose rustic summer retirement is perpetually interrupted by unwanted visitors, some of them invited by his spendthrift wife, and others brought in in a variety of other comic ways. Apart from a great deal of incidental bustle, the action hinges upon a fast-moving denouement—lawyer Barnard's decision to turn his house into an inn, his discovery that doing so means allowing the young Erast access to his daughter, the sudden threat to Barnard of punishment for killing the king's stag and Erast's equally sudden removal of that threat, and Barnard's gift of the house as a wedding present to the young couple. The treatment of these events in Vanbrugh's version is identical to that in Dancourt, except that in *The Country House* there is no longer a hint that Barnard and his son Dorant will be reconciled.

The greatest number of alterations in the French original, of course, are Vanbrugh's changes in language—his making the colorless French both more detailed and more vivid, and his elimination of references that might not be clear to an English audience. But the alteration of most moment, the one that most affects the dramatic force of the play, comes in the central character. It is easy to see in the changed Barnard two of the prime ingredients that had gone into his predecessors: with Sir John Brute he shares an antimarital bias not to be found in *La Maison de Campagne;* with Sir Tunbelly Clumsey and Sir Polidorus Hogstye, a lively interest in finances. The frugality of Barnard is, to be sure, an intensification of his French original, as in the added speech, "Is it so hard to comprehend, that he who spends a Shilling and receives but Six-pence, must be ruin'd in the End?" (II, 222). But his misogyny is entirely new. Vanbrugh's man insults his wife before the servant Lisett and finds the Marquis's praise of Madam Barnard as "the best Woman in the world" too fulsome for a gentlemanly reply. "Rot me if she be, Sir," he growls. And his offer to Erast to throw his wife in with his daughter as part of the bargain is worthy of Sir John Brute; and so is the triplet with which he ends the play: "My House dispos'd of, which was the Cause of Strife,/ I now may hope to lead a happy Life,/ If I can part with my ingaging Wife" (II, 231).

III   The Pilgrim

For the third of his alterations, this time of an English original, Vanbrugh turned to Fletcher's intrigue comedy *The Pilgrim* (1621). Unlike his earlier translations, however, and his original plays, *The Pilgrim* scarcely deserves the name comedy, except as a representative of the Renaissance type that brought a serious action to a happy close. The best of the comic scenes are undoubtedly those in the madhouse, although we no longer even smile at what the seventeenth century thought hilarious. As might be expected, Richard Steele found the bedlam episodes so offensive that he wrote a *Spectator* essay (March 26, 1711) to criticize "the false taste the Town is in" in approving those parts of *The Pilgrim*, particularly the first scene at the madhouse. Vanbrugh was so far from Steele's sentimental cast when he "corrected" the play for Dryden's benefit, however, that he actually enlarged the bedlam episodes; he added a Mad Taylor in Act IV, scene 2, and inserted a scene near the end of Act V in which Alphonso is released from the asylum.

The other alterations are largely minor adjustments in characters and in language, most of them in an attempt to make the play more comic and to turn nearly all of Fletcher's blank verse and rhymed tetrameter into prose. The plot meanders on unchanged, relying endlessly on disguises and long-winded speeches for much of its effect. Alphonso would marry his daughter Alinda to the outlaw

Roderigo, but she loves Pedro, the mortal enemy of both the father
and the outlaw. Pedro disguises himself as a pilgrim in order to be
near Alinda, and she assumes a series of disguises in order to join
him—first as a boy; then as a "she fool"; an old woman; and, finally,
as a shepherdess. Alphonso, pursuing her, is driven to distraction by
her servant Juletta, is beaten in the madhouse, and is finally reconciled to her union with Pedro. Roderigo and Pedro, meanwhile,
become friends and in the last scene are promised a pardon by the
governor.

Vanbrugh's changes in language fall into two general categories:
he tends to add words and phrases that relate to sexual activity and
to eliminate those that refer to "nasty" bodily functions. For example, when Alphonso asks what the Pilgrim wants, Vanbrugh adds "a
Wench" as one of the choices; and, when the four Peasants talk of
the outlaws, Vanbrugh gives them more realistic and explicit language: "They have robb'd me thrice," says one. "Me five times,"
says the other, "my Daughter fifty; tho' to give 'em their due, they
ne're take any thing from her, but what she can very well spare."
Fletcher's use of four letter Anglo-Saxonisms, however, is modestly
tempered; two or three "fart's" are silenced, for instance, and
"snotty-nos'd scab" becomes "saucy young Dog."

It is in the personages of the play, however, that the more important alterations are made. Vanbrugh enlarges the role of the drunk-
en porter and adds an enlivening stutter to the servant who reports
his mistress's flight through the garden. And he cuts a number of
sentimental passages, especially those in the speeches of Pedro and
Roderigo, that deal with reconciliation, honor, bravery, and the
like. Most altered of the characters, of course, is Alphonso; for, in
Fletcher's version, he is more serious and sympathetic, more a
victim and less a villain. His speeches in Act V, scene 5, of Vanbrugh's version, ally him, as a matter of fact, with Sir Tunbelly
Clumsey and with Barnard in his profane and grudging agreement
to accept his daughter's union. There is nothing in the Jacobean
original to suggest Alphonso's "I had a Daughter once with just such
a young whorish Leer as that" (II, 139) and "*Pedro's* a Dog, and if I
cou'd hang him, I wou'd. But since I can't, I'll be reveng'd another
way: He shall marry the Whore" (II, 140). The line of descent from
Clumsey, Brute, and Barnard is clear enough; and the pattern for
Vanbrugh's comic treatment of the father figure is solidly fixed.

IV The False Friend

Even less comic than *The Pilgrim* is the play that Vanbrugh next selected for translation, Alain René Lesage's *Le Traître Puni*, a love intrigue with a basic plot flaw that Vanbrugh left uncorrected. Apart from the coincidences common to the type of play, *Le Traître Puni* (renamed *The False Friend*) centered upon an unexpected return home by one of the characters. But the return was so poorly prepared for in the original and in the translation that the play was a failure because of it.

The anonymous author of *A Comparison Between the Two Stages* reflected the general reaction of the Drury Lane audience to *The False Friend:* Don Pedro, he observes, "having suddain news brought him of his Fathers approaching Death, he resolves to go immediately there, to take his blessing before he dy'd, and to pay him his filial Acknowledgments. The Journey was to last several Days. . . ." In the meantime, Don John attempts to rape Pedro's wife and is prevented by Don Guzman, formerly her lover. At this moment, says the anonymous critic, Don Pedro "comes in with incredible surprize. My Objection is, How [Pedro] can enter here? His Journey was to last several Days, nor was it feign'd; not many Hours had laps'd since his departure, and we hear of no Interruption by the way to cause him to turn back. Without doubt the Audience thought they have taken their leaves of him, unless some unexpected Accident had happen'd to him: Therefore I conclude his return in this Scene is unseasonable and forc'd for the Surprize." Nor was there the least hint, the critic complains, "that his Journey was a pretence, nor of any hindrance he met with by the way; which might easily have been done. . . ."[3]

In his plays, generally, however, Vanbrugh was not quick to see incongruities that might easily have been corrected. Loveless might have been given a motive for going to London, for example, or Amanda a reason for inviting Berinthia. Lady Fancyfull's improbable scheme in the denouement of *The Provok'd Wife* might easily have been prepared for a bit earlier in the play, and Dick Amlet's ten thousand pounds could readily have been foreshadowed. A playwright who treasured verisimilitude of action—as Vanbrugh obviously did not—would not have been likely to choose to remodel *The Pilgrim*, a play that relies heavily upon the improbable likelihood that costume changes can keep fathers, friends, and lovers from recognizing one another.   In order to enliven the action and to underscore the moral of *The False Friend*, Vanbrugh made a number of changes in the personages. The character of Leonora, for example, is made even more virtuous and noble than in the original, and Don John is transformed from an attractive rake to a sinister villain. In the original, Don André had been the false friend who attempts a rape and then plans a murder to conceal that attempt. Vanbrugh, however, changed the name from Don André to Don John, very likely remembering Molière's professional seducer Dom Juan, and gave his renamed character more of the latter's villainous traits. Where Don André had caught from his rival's interest in Leonora a renewed interest himself, Vanbrugh's John reveals a new depth of evil in the added lines, "The Fool has so provok'd me by his threat'ning, that I believe I shall have a Stroke at his Mother, before I think my self even with him" (II, 163). And there are many more indications of the translator's inclination to turn Don André into Dom Juan, primarily the addition of oaths and coarse language.

Nevertheless, in the event that the audience might mistake his alterations as a concession to Collier, Vanbrugh added an epilogue advocating rape ("There's wond'rous Charms in Vig'rous Execution" [II, 204]) and a prologue, directed to the "Dread Reformers of an Impious Age," that was heavy with irony and that reiterated Vanbrugh's defense in "Vindication" that comedy effects morality where sermons fail: "W'ave gentler Stratagems, which may succeed;/ We'll tickle 'em where you wou'd make 'em Bleed;/ In Sounds less harsh, we'll teach 'em to Obey; . . . / And steal their Immorality away" (II, 157).

The other change of note is a larger role for the servants in *The False Friend*. Lopez is changed from the relatively colorless Mogicon into the type of Sganarelle, Dom Juan's bold-mouthed, chicken-hearted, but clever valet, and Lopez is given a great many additional lines and a whole scene in which he courts Jacinta. In it, Vanbrugh captures his character in a single vignette: Lopez cannot sleep without dreaming of being beaten; his long-winded courtship of Jacinta finally bores her; and he ends in a soliloquy designed for the coarsest palate in the pit. Jacinta, in turn, is given a new scene (Act IV, scene 1) in which to display more fully Vanbrugh's conception of her character. Among all Vanbrugh's stage personages, her nearest relative is Madamoiselle; for, like her French cousin, she seeks only to bring fire and tinder together, to put Don Guzman and Leonora to bed with as much dispatch as possible. "Your Mistriss is now Marry'd, Sir, consider that. She has chang'd her Situation," she tells him, "and so must you your Battery. Attack a Maid Gently, a Wife Warmly, and be as rugged with a Widdow as you can" (II, 188). From a necessary adjunct to an intrigue plot, Jacinta grows into another of those troublesome Vanbrugh creations who are too light for tragedy and too dark for farce. Like the changes in Don John, those in Jacinta move the play farther from sentimentality and closer to the realism that the dramatist had established as his comic stock in trade.

V   The Confederacy

The Confederacy, the play with which Captain Vanbrugh chose to open the first full season of the new Queen's Theatre, Haymarket, is the most intricately plotted that he ever undertook to write or translate. In adapting Dancourt's *Bourgeoises à la Mode* for the English stage, he retained the double plot, the middle class setting, and the deus ex machina ending; but he made changes more far-reaching than those in any of his other adaptations. He not only speeds up the action and makes it more farcical, but also puts in italics Dancourt's satire of middle class mores and morals. As a consequence, the play comes closer than any of his other adapted ones to originality; it has most often been praised with *The Relapse* and *The Provok'd Wife* as one of his three comic masterpieces; and it was the third most frequently performed Vanbrugh play in the eighteenth century, appearing on stage forty-four times during his life. In the nineteenth century Hazlitt approved it as "a comedy of infinite contrivance and intrigue, with a matchless spirit of impudence . . . . a fine careless *exposé* of heartless want of principle; for there is no anger or severity against vice expressed in it. . . ."[4] W. C. Ward, Vanbrugh's first modern editor, ranked *The Confederacy* not only as the happiest of his translations but—more important—as the most brilliant of all his works.[5]

The plot, to be sure, remains largely the same as in *Les Bourgeoises à la Mode;* however, Vanbrugh tightens the construction and introduces new scenes in new locations that give a fast-paced Elizabethan flavor to the action. Two characters serve as wellsprings for the play's forward movement: Dick Amlet, the rakish son of a street peddlar, assumes a colonel's disguise in order to pursue the wealthy Corinna Gripe. Corinna's stepmother Clarissa is in perpetual pursuit of money in order to buy the appearance of quality, and she will all but sacrifice her virtue to obtain it. Dick's quest is complicated by Corinna's unfriendly father; by his own doting mother, who cannot understand why he must keep his relationship to her a secret; and by his greedy servant Brass, who fully intends to share in the fortune that Dick will gain. Clarissa Gripe's pursuit of quality is complicated by her husband's greed, which she hopes to circumvent by a series of stratagems that includes the plan that Flippanta (her servant) proposes in order to turn Gripe's and Moneytrap's lust for the other's wife into profit for the women. At the denouement, the wives' plot is revealed, but only after they have extracted several hundred pounds from their husbands; Dick's disguise is pierced, and his hopes for Corinna are endangered—until Mrs. Amlet announces that he is to have ten thousand pounds with which to begin the life of a country gentleman.

With a multitude of minor details, Vanbrugh adjusts this French original into a purely English production. The French tone of *The Country House*, his translation most like *The Confederacy* in plot and character, has disappeared; his characters are all honest English folk; not even a French servant betrays the play's Gallic origin. The middle class air of *Les Bourgeoises á la Mode* is reduced a social benchmark by Vanbrugh's enlargement of the servants' roles. So thoroughly do they dominate the action, as a matter of fact, and so much are Dick Amlet and his mother the pivotal point of half the plot, that *The Confederacy* deserves to be called *The Beggar's Opera* of manners comedy. Dick Amlet and Brass, master and servant, are only one step removed from the low class school boys and rakes they once were. "When we were Fellow-Prentices," says Brass, "tho' I was your Senior, you made me open the Shop, clean my Master's shoes, cut last at Dinner, and eat all the Crust. In our sins too, I must own you still kept me under; you soar'd up to Adultery with our Mistriss, while I was at humble Fornication with the Maid. Nay, in our Punishments, you still made good your Post; for when once upon a time I was sentenced but to be Whip'd, I cannot deny but you were condemn'd to be Hang'd" (III, 57). Dick's mother, Mrs. Amlet, the source of much of the play's farcical action, is no more than a street peddlar (although she proves to be an unusually wealthy one) whose husband was hanged for church robbery.

Gripe and Moneytrap, the bubbled husbands, are mere scriveners—copy clerks with one foot in the middle class. For Gripe's wife Clarissa, however, the family's place in the caste system is a perpetual source of comic distress; and her distress is the wellspring for the other half of the action. "Is it not a most horrible Thing," she says, "that I should be but a Scrivener's Wife? . . . don't you think Nature design'd me for something, *plus elevée*" (III, 19). The conflict between status quo and aspirations is best seen in the famous quarrel scene between husband and wife:

CLAR. And as this kind of Life, so soft, so smooth, so agreeable, must needs invite a vast deal of Company to partake of it, 'twill be necessary to have the decency of a Porter at our Door, you know.

GRIPE. A Porter——a Scrivener have a Porter, Madam?

CLAR. Positively, a Porter.

GRIPE. Why no Scrivener since *Adam* ever had a Porter, Woman!

CLAR. You will therefore be renown'd in Story, for having the first, my Life (III, 56).

Flippanta, whose role was enlarged to suit Mrs. Bracegirdle's talents, is generalissimo of all the plots; but she is withal a mere servant in the Gripe family with many grasping ambitions of her own.

The single most effective and delightful enlargement of a character is that of Mrs. Amlet. Although Vanbrugh retains the deus ex machina ending in which she produces ten thousand pounds to bring the play to a happy close, he adds two scenes which foreshadow her possession of wealth. The first, Act I, scene 1, introduces her considerable trade with both the "great folks" and the citizens; the second, Act III, scene 1, discovers Dick's search of her strong box for cash, notes, or bank bills, a fact that hints, at least, at the likelihood of her having money. In this scene, furthermore, she continues to be curiously uninterested in his pursuit of wealth, an additional suggestion, perhaps, that she is the possessor of a fortune of her own. What does interest her, of course, is that her dear Dick should return a little of his mother's love; and she cares nothing for quality or about other people's fortunes.

In Vanbrugh's hands, Mrs. Amlet becomes something entirely
new on the English stage—the fondly doting mother who is so much
in love with her son's good looks—his shape, his nose, his cherry
lip—that nothing matters but his success and her vicarious delight
in it. Like Hoyden's nurse, Mrs. Amlet lavishes unwelcome affection upon her favorite until he is ready for that reason alone to
disown her. It is not, as one writer has suggested, that Dick's conduct toward his mother is morally questionable and even ruthless,[6]
but rather that the exaggeration of the mother for comic effect calls
for a like exaggeration of the son. Each becomes a figure of farce in
the classic chase pattern but the roles are reversed: the woman
pursues and praises; the man is in full flight.

As in Vanbrugh's two original plays, he laid stress in his adaptation upon exposing the selfish motives of most of mankind, whether
quality or citizens. What satire he employs in *The Confederacy* is
more upon the rough and tumble urgency with which some of them
pursue wealth and love than upon their hypocrisy in concealing it.
All but the husbands and Corinna are aimed solely by greed, and
the exceptions are those persons urged by frankly expressed sexual
desires. Indeed, what appears out of the smoke and dust of the
actions is *The Provok'd Wife* theme with a vengeance—that marriage is at best a leaky vessel, especially when entered into by the
woman out of ambition and by the man out of lust. In place of
Heartfree's devotion and Bellinda's common sense to restore to
marriage an optimistic note, there is only Corinna's faint hope:
"What's mine is yours, and when our Estates are put together, I
don't doubt but we shall do as well as the best of 'em" (III, 72). The
specific instance of one gross husband, Sir John Brute, is enlarged
throughout *The Confederacy* into a generalization for all husbands.
The most telling speech (Act II, scene 1) is comic, to be sure, and
delivered by Flippanta (a saucy servant) for a specific purpose (to
encourage Moneytrap to pursue Mrs. Gripe); therefore, it cannot be
taken as the playwright's considered judgment. Yet Flippanta's
phrases describing husbands—"Little, peeking, creeping, sneaking,
stingy, covetous, cowardly, dirty, cuckoldy Things. . . . A Dog in a
Manger, snarling and biting, to starve Gentlemen with good
Stomachs. . . . A Bag without Money—an empty Bottle—dead
Small-Beer" (III, 33)—strongly reinforce the antimarriage atmosphere that is developed throughout much of the comedy.

Side by side with the antimarital thrust of the play, however, is a positive statement that approves a middle course of life like that that Bellinda had proposed as an alternative to the ambitious search for a husband of rank. Corinna's willingness to accept a more modest way of life in the country, although it is found in Dancourt's play, is set off more sharply from Clarissa's pursuit of a life of quality by the satiric additions Vanbrugh made. The most significant of the new passages is Clarissa's speech about conspicuous consumption: "Quality always distinguishes it self; and therefore, as the Mechanick People buy things, because they have occasion for 'em, you see Women of Rank always buy things, because they have not occasion for 'em. Now, there, *Flippanta*, you see the difference between a Woman that has breeding, and one that has none (III, 27). The addition is little enough by itself, perhaps, but taken together with Vanbrugh's numerous references to money and his selection of the names *Gripe* and *Moneytrap* for his dupes, it is clear that the message of *The Confederacy* is like that in *Aesop* of the country mouse at court warning against greed: "Since every Man shou'd have his due,/ I own, Sir, I'm oblig'd to you,/ For your Intentions at your Board./ But Pox upon your Courtly Crew——" (II, 31).

VI   The Mistake

The last of Vanbrugh's adaptations was his turning into prose *Le Depit Amoureux* (1656), a comedy that Molière had taken from *Interesse* (1581), a play by the Italian Nicolo Secchi.[7] Once again the English version departed very little from the original; and *The Mistake*, as Vanbrugh titled it, suffers from the same complicated and unreal plot that plagued *Le Depit Amoureux*. Although Vanbrugh changed the names from French to Spanish in order to exploit the current interest in the War of the Spanish Succession, in which England was now involved, he left Molière's scenes uncut and in precisely the same arrangement as before.

The action centers about the *daughter* of Don Alvarez, who all her life has pretended to be his *son* Camillo. The complications begin in earnest when "Camillo" falls in love with her sister Leonora's suitor Don Lorenzo. After a series of night meetings in which she pretends to be Leonora, Camillo marries Lorenzo in secret. Consequently, when a second suitor—Don Carlos—learns of Leonora's supposed marriage, he charges her with betraying him. The resultant scene of their separation and reconciliation (with the servants' imitation of the two lovers) is the most delightful in the play. The truth of Camillo's birth is discovered and she is honorably united with Don Lorenzo.

Once again Vanbrugh turned his attention from the plot to the characters and the mood of the play by adding lively and occasionally gross detail where the French version had been pedestrian, by diminishing long speeches, and by increasing the amount of farcical action, especially in the servants' scenes. Where Molière's maidservant, for instance, urges the lover in Act I with a general observation about jealousy, Vanbrugh's Jacinta waxes specific: "When you suspect a Woman's falling off, you fall a plaguing her to bring her on again, attack her with Reason, and a sour Face; udslife, Sir, attack her with a Fiddle, double your good Humour,——give her a Ball,——powder your Perriwig at her,——let her cheat you at Cards a little, and I'll warrant all's right again" (III, 89). In Act V, scene 1, Molière's servant Mascarille repeats his master's instructions as they prepare to enter the house, simply telling him to bring the lantern and a few weapons. But, in *The Mistake*, Lopez is given the kind of colorful detail that delighted Vanbrugh: "Therefore make haste, *Lopez*," he tells himself, "prepare every thing necessary, Three Pair of Pocket-Pistols, Two wide-mouth'd Blunderbusses, some Six Ells of Sword-Blade, and a Couple of dark Lanthorns" (III, 120).

The best illustration of Vanbrugh's alterations comes in Act IV, the famous lovers' quarrel. He adds specific stage business that is only implied in Molière: Don Carlos goes off and returns, he twitches Leonora's picture from his breast, and she "Breaks a Bracelet from her Arm" as they return their gifts to each other. The servants are even more demonstrative: Sancho throws a deck of cards at Jacinta and tears off her headclothes; she responds by pulling off his wig; and both run back to their masters. The farce reaches its climax when Sancho returns Jacinto's handkerchief, but first blows his nose in it, and she leaps about his neck and pleads for him to beat her. An acted version of Molière's comedy might be expected to develop some of the same stage business that Vanbrugh proposes for this scene; but the fact that he himself envisioned it, without leaving that task to the actors, and did it so very clearly and in such lively detail, is an additional demonstration of his peculiar genius for investing borrowed plays with a vitality of action (and a comic English vocabulary) that enabled them to make the perilous transition from one language and one culture to another.

Vanbrugh's efforts in behalf of *The Mistake* helped it to an opening run of six performances. In order to assure a week of full houses he buttressed the fourth performance with "Italian songs by Bononcini and other Masters," and he enlived his own sixth night—when, as author, he received the profits—with dancing by de Barques, Mrs. Elford, Mlle. de Noisy; with "a new *Chacone* by Mrs. Bruce"; and with a "Scotch Dance by Mrs. Bicknell." Despite its early success, however, *The Mistake* proved to be a failure during Vanbrugh's lifetime; for it had only eight more performances after January 1706. John Downes thought the translation witty and diverting, but he predicted that it would "scarce be Enroll'd a Stock-Play." More recently, John Wilcox has praised it as the "first good acting translation of Molière into English" and as "more natural and more amusing than the original."[8]

VII *A Translator's Achievements*

In *The Mistake* and in the other adaptations, we can recognize Vanbrugh's achievement as a translator as well as his vision of the comic universe. What he did with the French, first of all, was to make it English, to give it enough life to succeed on an English stage even when the locale and the atmosphere—as in *The Country House*—continued to be foreign. Next, he added a new vitality of language and action: he enriched his adaptations with vivid and sometimes grotesque detail—oaths, odd catalogues, colorful names, exuberant analogies, and figures of speech—and he always sought the scene change and physical action that would give Shakespearean life to a more staid original.

Finally, he expanded or created from whole cloth a set of memorable "humours" characters, most of them servants and all of them strongly marked English types: the abusive Sir Polidorus Hogstye, the marriage-hating Mr. Barnard, the stuttering servant of *The Pilgrim*, the cowardly Lopez and the libertine Jacinta of *The False Friend*, a whole set of stage originals in *The Confederacy*, and the bold and lively Jacinta and Sancho of *The Mistake*. The high blown sentiments of romance drew Captain Vanbrugh like the song of the Sirens—as can be seen in three of his six adaptations and in parts of *The Relapse* and *The Provok'd Wife*—but, in striking for the taste of the pit and the gallery, he found the course that could best rescue his plays—the addition of those farcical elements that have ever since been seen as most characteristic of "Brother Van."

CHAPTER 6

The Posthumous Vanbrugh

A^T the time of his death in March 1726, Sir John Vanbrugh had already left a powerful imprint upon the body and soul of England. From Northumberland and Durham in the North to Somerset and Dorset in the Southwest, his great country houses were still rising and filling out the lines that his hand had sketched months and years before. Some of them, like Eastbury, that continued upward for many more years, served as a kind of living and growing memorial to the architect's genius. In like manner, Vanbrugh was kept alive on the London stage; for a burst of performances of all eight of his comedies occurred in the months immediately following his demise, and a steady procession of his best plays were on stage throughout the rest of the eighteenth century. There was even a new Vanbrugh comedy, *The Provok'd Husband,* in January 1728, which, though revised and completed by Colley Cibber, displayed here and there Vanbrugh's farcical vignettes, his lively "humours" characters, and his splendid quarrelling scenes.

If Vanbrugh's reputation declined in the nineteenth century, with only a rare appearance of one of his plays in the theater, the great essay writers of the century—Charles Lamb, William Hazlitt, Leigh Hunt, and Thomas Macaulay—kept his name alive; there were editions by Hunt, W. C. Ward, and A. E. H. Swaen; and individual comedies were reprinted in the stream of many-volumed anthologies that formed the century's chief contribution to British drama. But, in the twentieth century, the scholars evinced interest in Vanbrugh's plays and letters, which were edited and reedited; studies of his architectural accomplishments began to appear in superbly illustrated volumes; and his contributions to comic drama began to be analyzed in a growing number of articles and books by serious students of Restoration and eighteenth century literature.

133

Outside the narrow world of academe, however, Vanbrugh has
once again become something of a popular success—as success is
marked in these days of mass media—with a contemporary musical
version of *The Relapse* called *Virtue in Danger* (1963); a film with
Relapsian characters, called *Lock Up Your Daughters* (1969); ap-
pearances by the dramatist-architect in two television series that
have played extensively in England and America—*Civilisation*, in
which his work on stage and in stone is used to exemplify the
paradise of the amateur that was the eighteenth century; and *The
First Churchills*, the story of the Marlboroughs, in one episode of
which Vanbrugh and the Duchess exchange pleasantries about his
buildings and his morals. There have been brief stage revivals in
England of *The Relapse* (1947, 1966) and of *The Confederacy* (1964).
To crown all, the world-famous Tyrone Guthrie Theatre in Min-
neapolis opened its 1972 season in July with a three play repertoire,
including none other than *The Relapse;* and Vanbrugh's play was
puffed in the company's promotion campaign as "a full-blooded and
more-than-slightly bawdy comedy in the style of *Tom Jones. . . .*"

I *The Orphan Muse*

It is impossible to know quite what Vanbrugh intended to do with
the fragment of a comedy that found its way at his death into the
hands of his old friend Colley Cibber. He mentions nothing of *A
Journey to London* in any of his letters, and the manuscript itself
seems to have disappeared soon after Cibber gave it to J. Watts for
printing. There are but two accounts of the play's existence, and
neither is very revealing. Cibber, of course, is the earlier and more
detailed source of information; for, when he published the original
together with his revision, *The Provok'd Husband*, he explained the
reason for doing so: "In my last Conversation with [Sir John], (which
chiefly turn'd upon what he had done towards a Comedy) he excus'd
his not shewing it me, 'till he had review'd it, confessing the Scenes
were yet undigested, too long, and irregular, particularly in the
Lower Characters [.] I have but one Excuse for publishing, what he
never design'd should come into the World, as it then was, *viz.* I
had no other way of taking those many Faults to myself, which may
be justly found in my presuming to finish it."[1] Although Richard
Cumberland's account adds nothing to Cibber's, Cumberland remembered many years later a comment by George Bubb
Dodington, "that Vanbrugh told him, that he had sketched out some

loose scenes, which, in quantity, were enough for a comedy, but which had no plan or properties of an entire composition in them."[2]

The structure of Vanbrugh's "loose scenes" is as episodic as that of *The Relapse.* Act I introduces those involved in the minor plot, the members of the Headpiece family: first, through Uncle Richard's soliloquy and conversation about their coming to London; second, through their arrival at the lodgings of Mrs. Motherly. The second act is devoted to bringing in the major plot, the Lord and Lady Loverule debate about her irregular course of life. Act III returns to the Headpiece family and their abortive trip to the theater; and Act IV displays Lady Loverule on the morning after a gambling bout and brings the Headpiece family to her for a visit. Unlike *The Relapse,* of course, there is no resolution and no indication of how Vanbrugh might have brought it about except for his remark to Cibber that he intended to have Lord Loverule turn his lady out of doors, as the lord threatens to do in Act I, scene 1, and after.

Although *A Journey to London* is incomplete, it is possible to observe in the four finished acts some of the problems that faced Vanbrugh as he sought to form them into a coherent whole. Apart from the absence of an Act V to bring all complications to a resolution, the double plot is the chief weakness, because the two plots divide our attention, just as they did in *The Relapse* and in *Aesop,* and because the playwright does not offer much hope of bringing the two together. The entrance of the Headpiece family in Act IV is a bit of arrant legerdemain, and the existence outside the two families of two more separate sets of characters—Uncle Richard for one, and Sir Charles and Clarinda for the other—blurs the focus even more. Uncle Richard's monologue to open the play, although it accords with Vanbrugh's practice in *The Relapse* and *The Provok'd Wife,* is less effective than exposition through dialogue; and the elaborate description that Richard's servant James gives of the Headpiece entourage credits him with a memory (or an omniscience) that would tax the willing suspension of disbelief in any audience.

The Provok'd Husband was Cibber's attempt to deal with most of these plot flaws. By giving Lady Loverule (changed to Lady Townly) much more good sense and by shifting a share of the blame for her misconduct to Lord Loverule's uxoriousness, Cibber made her sentimental repentance more probable. At a single stroke he tied the four loose parts of Vanbrugh's story together by combining Uncle

Richard and Sir Charles into Mr. Manly and by making Clarinda into Lady Arabella's sister-in-law Grace. Thus Manly's courtship of Lady Grace bridges the gap between the comic subplot and the main plot. Although Cibber retained the soliloquy that opens the comedy, he assigned it instead to Lord Loverule (renamed Lord Townly), thus helping to make the major plot the more important of the two stories. Finally, Cibber gave to Manly the news of the Headpiece (now Wronghead) arrival in town and wisely left the details of their coming to the Wronghead servant, John Moody.

Not all of the changes made to produce *The Provok'd Husband*, however, were improvements upon *A Journey to London*. At first, of course, Cibber was wrongly damned as the author of the comic subplot and Vanbrugh was praised for the morality of the mainplot; but anyone familiar with the earlier work of the two men should have known which was which.[3] Even when the lower plot was properly credited to Vanbrugh, however, a comparison of the two published plays revealed to the world some considerable changes, especially the elimination of two fine scenes of farce—one in which the goose pie is stolen (Act I, scene 2) and Squire Humphrey, like one voice in a three part catch, repeats the melancholy news: "So, the poor Pye's quite gone then," and "It was a rare good Pye," and again "I had rather they had run away with heavy *George* than the Goose Pye. . . ." A second unfortunate omission was that of the scene in which Lady Headpiece and company return after their coach is upset. The irony of so dirty a return after so elaborate a going out is delicious. And Colonel Courtly's courageous report of his injuries ("Only a little wounded with some Pins I met with about your Ladyship . . . . my poor Hands were got once——I don't know where they were got" [III, 161].) makes him less the designing villain than he appears to be in *The Provok'd Husband*.

Vanbrugh, of course, had a better reason than Cibber did for including such a scene, along with James's and John Moody's earlier descriptions of the overloaded Headpiece coach on its way to London and Heavy George's account of the demise of that same vehicle at the hands of a sadistic carter named Dick. The architect's own rambling about from one great house to another in all kinds of weather lends a special reality to these passages. English roads were notoriously bad (the reader recalls Macaulay's anecdote of a coach and six disappearing from sight in the mud) and coach travel was extremely dangerous. In his December 1699 letter to Manchester, for example, Vanbrugh reported that the Duchess of Leeds had overturned while riding by torchlight, "and so desparately bruis'd, she has been at the brink of death with't" (IV, 5). Coincidentally, Mrs. Mary Porter, who played Lady Grace in the 1728 premiere of *The Provok'd Husband*, was herself so hurt a few months later by upsetting in a chaise that she was lost to the theater,[4] and not long afterward Vanbrugh's old friend Congreve received a mortal injury when his coach upset.

In the serious mainplot of *The Provok'd Husband*, Cibber's changes were so extensive that he made that portion of the play his own. Besides assigning a share of the blame to Lord Townly and improving his lady's character in order to achieve a sentimental denouement, Cibber modified the bawdy and the blunt speeches—especially those of Arabella—thus making the tone of these passages more genteel. Two scenes in particular Cibber found incompatible with his remodelled heroine: in deference to her newly found gentility, he virtually eliminated the degrading scene in which she first tricks and then outfaces Shortyard the mercer; and he excised entirely the scene in which Captain Toupee treats her with nauseous familiarity and then plays at dice with her.

Cibber's revisions produced a finished play, one that not only lifted his sagging reputation and the spirits of the Drury Lane company but also marked a significant revival of legitimate drama in the midst of a flurry of pantomime-farces. For those reasons alone, *The Provok'd Husband* is a more important accomplishment than *A Journey to London*. Yet Vanbrugh's fragment displays most of the characteristic features of his plays, and it represents in some ways the best accomplishment of his comic genius.

The language alone reveals Vanbrugh at his most inspired. Nowhere else in the farcical scenes of his original plays or adaptations is there such a wealth of comic detail, such catalogues of incongruous description and narrative, such a Rabelaisian effect of grotesque plenitude. The best of these passages are more laughter-provoking, surely, than their antecedents in *The Relapse, Aesop, The Country House,* and *The Confederacy.* Uncle Richard begins the barrage of exuberant nouns and adjectives with his soliloquy about Sir Francis Headpiece; and it is followed by James's recital of the Headpiece odyssey and equipage:

They'd have been here last Night, but that the old wheezy-belly Horse
tir'd, and the two fore-wheels came crash down at once in *Wagonrut*-Lane.
Sir, they were cruelly loaden. . . . Then Sir, for fear of a Famine, before
they shou'd get to the Baiting-place, there was such Baskets of Plumbcake,
Dutch-Gingerbread, Cheshire-Cheese, Naples-Biscuits, Maccaroons,
Neats-Tongues, and cold boyl'd Beef—and in case of Sickness, such Bottles
of Usquebaugh, Black-cherry Brandy, Cinamon-water, Sack, Tent, and
Strong beer, as made the old Coach crack again (III, 136–37).

James, to be sure, is given some of the best vocabulary in Vanbrugh's low comedy dictionary, but nearly everybody in the subplot
is allowed a rich complement of Anglo-Saxonisms. George reports
the death of the coach: "Before we were gotten to the Street end, a
great Lugger-headed Cart, with Wheels as thick as a good Brick
Wall, layd hawld of the Coach, and has pood it aw to Bits" (III, 143).
Miss Betty displays a rare skill in selecting phrases that aptly describe her glutton brother; and Sir Francis Headpiece delivers a
garrulous account of his day at Parliament that shows rustic innocence at its worst.

The major plot, too, has moments—as in Arabella's and Clarinda's
exchanges in Act II, scene 1—when Vanbrugh's fondness for provid-
ing illustrations and examples shows itself brilliantly. In the
Loverule story, however, the best passages are those of wit rather
than of comic detail. The outstanding example is, of course, the
scene just noted in which Lady Arabella outlines for Clarinda the
conversational joys of married life. The irony is given its powerful
comic force by the preceding exchange between Lord and Lady
Loverule over her late hours, her gambling, and her prodigal spend-
ing. Taking her cue from Arabella's account, Clarinda asks: "But in
such sort of Family Dialogues (tho' extreamly well for passing of
Time) don't there now and then enter some little witty sort of Bitterness?" Lady Arabella replies: "O yes; which don't do amiss at all;
a little something that's sharp, moderates the extream Sweetness of
matrimonial Society, which wou'd else perhaps be cloying. Tho' to
tell you the truth, *Clarinda*, I think we squeezed a little too much
Lemon into it . . ." (III, 149).

The characters of *A Journey to London* are only partially developed, to be sure, but most of them appear to be closely allied to
personages in Vanbrugh's earlier plays and translations. Francis
Headpiece, for example, is Sir Tunbelly Clumsey removed to London; his wife has a share in the ladies of *The Confederacy;* and Betty

is Hoyden with a younger brother. Martilla is the cast-off mistress that Lady Brute feared to become at Constant's hands, and Mrs. Motherly is Mrs. Amlet with rooms to rent. The predatory beaux and garrulous servants, too, find their antecedents in Vanbrugh's earlier works, but the servants are, in general, more rustic and more fully developed in the fragments of *A Journey to London*. Uncle Richard and Squire Humphrey stand alone in the subplot as Vanbrugh originals, even though the booby and the surly bachelor types had appeared frequently on the Restoration stage.

The married couple who comprise the main plot provide the greater challenge to our understanding of motivation. In place of the "humours" that control the characters of the minor plot, conflicting forces are at play in the man as well as in the woman; and a marital issue is at stake. Lord Loverule's long marriage has cured him of his earlier romantic belief that women are goodness personified: "The Pleasure is so great," he says, "in believing Women to be, what we wish them; that nothing but a long and sharp Experience can ever make us think them otherwise" (III, 153). He is now so far from that previous misconception that he is willing to abandon his dream of delight in marriage if he can only preserve his reputation. Even this meager hope, however, is frustrated, first by Lady Loverule's refusal to give up her late hours and her gambling; then by concrete evidence of her abuse of her creditors, and finally by the fulsome familiarity with which she is treated by Captain Toupee, her gambling companion. A man of moderation can have only one answer to these excesses, however uncomic it might be; and, by the end of his conversation with Sir Charles, Lord Loverule is prepared to take the final step, separation.

The central character in the serious major plot is, of course, Lady Loverule, another of Vanbrugh's intelligent, witty, but flawed heroines. Like Berinthia, her pursuit of pleasure is self-centered and whole-hearted; and, like Clarissa Gripe in *The Confederacy*, her special vices are gambling and fashionable living. "I doat upon Assemblies," she tells Clarinda, "adore Masquerades, my Heart bounds at a Ball; I love Play to distraction, Cards enchant me, and Dice—put me out of my little Wits—Dear, dear Hazard, what Music there is in the Rattle of the Dice, compared to a sleepy Opera!" (III, 149). Arabella has, as well, a good deal of Lady Brute's confidence in woman's wit and in her ability to win; but she has not that lady's caution or good luck. She baits her husband into threatening to lock her out, degrades herself by squabbling with Mr. Shortyard and by falsely accusing him of lying, and offers Lord Loverule the penultimate insult by permitting Captain Toupee's coarse familiarities in her dressing room.

With his usual concern for creating believable women, Vanbrugh provided his audience with a glimpse into Lady Loverule's life before marriage as well as with a clue to her philosophy. That philosophy emerges in the debate with her husband that opens Act II. Her faults, she argues, are natural ones; and their "mending" is as unnatural as the weaning of infants or the fasting of religious folk. No matter what her conduct, in fact, it cannot make her husband look foolish; for, "If Heav'n has made you otherwise, that won't be in my Power." Hence he, too, she implies, is controlled by deterministic forces that cannot be altered. Her philosophy seems to be a rationalization, however, for the principle that truly guides her life is that the approval of the polite world is more to be sought than the moderation her husband urges.

Lady Arabella's life in her father's house is only suggested, to be sure, but it appears to have been sufficiently retired for her new freedom after marriage to make her giddy. Her father, she reveals in her soliloquy in Act II, scene 1, so doubted women's judgment that "he did not think it fit they shou'd be trusted with Pin-money, and so wou'd not let [Lord Loverule] settle one Penny upon his poor Wife . . ." (III, 148). Now her spendthrift habits have served to confirm her father's evaluation. She seems, like Lady Brute, to have married for social advancement rather than for love; for she regards her husband as a necessary evil, tells Sir Charles that she doesn't mind if her husband has woman visitors, and treats Lord Loverule with contempt in front of Captain Toupee.

Although the two characters thus outlined are left incomplete, Vanbrugh has clearly prepared for the inevitability of their separation. He may have conceived an ending that would punish Lady Arabella, vindicate her spouse, and still achieve the comic equilibrium needed for the genre that he chose. Such a denouement seems most unlikely, however, and it is virtually certain that Vanbrugh's failure to complete *A Journey to London* arose from his realization that comic drama could not sustain the treatment he envisioned and that tragic drama demanded a far more serious issue than a wife's late hours and compulsive gambling. There are a number of morals in the play, to be sure, lessons in social conduct to suit the new sobriety of the era—a treatise on the evils of city life, examples in Clarinda and Sir Charles of well-regulated living, an outburst against primogeniture, and some Popeian levity about prudes and coquettes. But the issue of habitual gambling, on which the major plot turns, must somehow be given a comic twist if the play is to be rescued both from the impending abyss of permanent separation and from the sentimental rose garden of reconciliation that was the play's ultimate fate.

It is pleasant, in the midst of this uncertainty about the play's resolution, to recall how easily the chain of matrimony hung about Vanbrugh himself, how well regulated his married life appears to have been, and how readily even card playing was made a part of his agreeable life. Lady Vanbrugh, at least, had learned the lesson of the Loverule's; for, in the middle of Sir John's letter of invitation to Jacob Tonson on November 29, 1719, to share some of his wife's good Yorkshire housewifery is this charming postcript: "& if you will make one at cards as I understand you have often done, with much finer Ladys then I am I give you my word that I will neither cheat nor wrangle. Your Servant, Hariot V." (IV, 123).

II *Dramatic Reputation*

Fame is a good deal like a shuttlecock, as somebody has said; and, the harder the returns, the livelier the game. While Vanbrugh lived, his reputation as a dramatist was established almost exclusively by the praise of wits and critics on the one side of the net and the condemnation of the moralizers on the other. The Collier Controversy, as a matter of fact, set a critical tone and a point of view that was to last well into the eighteenth century; for Jeremy Collier's followers bitterly condemned the comedies as immoral, profane, and irregular. The wits of the early eighteenth century, on the other hand, tended to praise Vanbrugh as either a man—a sweet-natured gentleman, a genius, a wit, and the like—or a playwright who produced agreeable, easy, laughing comedy. With the exception of Collier and Colley Cibber, however, nobody in the century troubled himself with a serious analysis of Vanbrugh's comic accomplishment. Samuel Johnson's decision to omit Sir John from *The Lives of the Poets* reflected as much a judgment upon his bawdy as upon his dramaturgy, and it represented an attitude that was to prevail until William Hazlitt, Charles Lamb, and Leigh Hunt began the nineteenth century resurrection of the comedy of manners.

The greatest critical interest in Vanbrugh during the eighteenth century came, predictably, while his plays were popular on the stage. From the first performance of *The Relapse* in November 1696 and on, they were regularly produced. In the 1730's and 1740's they reached the peak of their popularity; thereafter, they declined steadily, for only *The Relapse, The Provok'd Wife, The Confederacy,* and *The Mistake* were produced with any frequency.[5] During the first half of the eighteenth century, Vanbrugh's contemporary men of letters linked his name frequently with the names of Etherege, Wycherley, and Congreve; but they found him to be their superior in the creation of familiar stage conversation.

Charles Gildon was the first to place him on the same level of wit as Wycherley and Etherege, above all other modern writers of comedy: "The easiness, and at the same time, force of the Conversation of his Plays are such, that none else can stand in Competition with him."[6] In 1719, Giles Jacob praised his "great sprightliness of Conversation," his easy dialogue, and his justly drawn characters; and he then linked him with Congreve as the preferred modern writer of comedy.[7] On at least three occasions Pope praised Vanbrugh's ear for conversation: the poet is reported to have defended Sir John to Swift as "the most easy careless writer and companion in the world" and to have named him as one of the four English writers (with Ben Jonson, Roger L'Estrange, and Congreve) who might be considered as authorities for familiar English dialogue.[8] The most detailed praise of Vanbrugh's gift for language, of course, appeared in Colley Cibber's 1740 *Apology*—the most thorough and accurate evaluation that was to be afforded Sir John for the next eighty years:

Though, to write much, in a little time, is no Excuse for writing ill; yet Sir *John Vanbrugh's* Pen, is not be be a little admir'd, for its Spirit, Ease, and Readiness, in producing Plays so fast, upon the Neck of one another; for, notwithstanding this quick Dispatch, there is a clear and lively Simplicity in his Wit, that neither wants the Ornament of Learning, nor has the least Smell of the Lamp in it. . . . There is something so catching to the Ear, so easy to the Memory, in all he writ, that it has been observ'd, by all the Actors of my Time, that the Style of no Author whatsoever, gave their Memory less trouble. . . .[9]

The various histories of drama and poetry (by David Baker, Thomas Davies, Charles Dibdin, and others) that came from the presses in the second half of the eighteenth century tended to rely heavily upon Cibber's estimate. Among the men of letters of this period, however, who had praise for the dramatist were Henry Fielding, who ranked him with Shakespeare and Jonson in *Pasquin* and who named him with Congreve in *Tom Jones* as a playwright who copied nature. Oliver Goldsmith put him with Cibber as the last writers to have presented laughing, low comedy. Edmund Burke praised his wit, humor, and characterization; but Burke followed Collier in condemning his immorality and irregular plots. Richard Sheridan paid him the compliment of adaptation, and Horace Walpole threw out an occasional approving sally in his letters.

In the nineteenth century, Vanbrugh's comedies were only rarely staged. Charles Lamb, as a matter of fact, began his famous essay with the melancholy declaration that "The artificial Comedy, or Comedy of manners, is quite extinct on our stage."[10] But Lamb's defense of the Restoration comic world as unreal—as a land "of cuckoldry—the Utopia of gallantry"—although it may to some degree have described Etherege, Wycherley, and Congreve, could not apply to the farcical realism of the low characters who took larger space in Vanbrugh's scenes. It is impossible, furthermore, to square the tempting of Amanda and Lady Brute and the problems of marital adjustment that Vanbrugh probed in all three original plays with Lamb's dismissal of manners comedy as amoral, "a passing pageant, where we should sit as unconcerned at the issues, for life or death, as at a battle of the frogs and mice."[11]

William Hazlitt, whose lecture on Wycherley, Congreve, Vanbrugh, and Farquhar had appeared four years earlier, offered a better judgment than Lamb. Far from dismissing manners comedy as unreal, he insisted that "the stage must be copied from real life"; and he agreed with Vanbrugh in "Vindication" that exposing vice and folly on the stage was as necessary as exposing it from the pulpit.[12] Hazlitt's greater attention was given, however, to the literary qualities of Vanbrugh's plays in which he found not the easy conversation that had intrigued the wits of the early eighteenth century but a fund of ludicrous description and—above all—the execution of "the most difficult and rapid theatrical movements at a moment's warning"—the ingenious extrication of a character whose cause is apparently hopeless. Although Hazlitt judged Vanbrugh to be little concerned about his characters' motivations or about the construction of plot, his recognition of the playwright's skill in building the well-made scene is both new and timely.

The second lift to Vanbrugh's reputation, by Leigh Hunt, was no sooner given than it was counterbalanced by the most able controversialist of the nineteenth century, Thomas Babington Macaulay. In Hunt's edition of plays by Wycherley, Congreve, Vanbrugh, and Farquhar, he included critical-biographical essays about each; and the general tenor of his essays was that the Restoration period needed the chastisement offered by its comic drama. The evaluation of Vanbrugh is especially discerning: "His character as a comic writer is clear and obvious. It is straightforward, cheerful, confident, and robust; . . . not over-nice in its decorums, not giving too much credit to conventional virtues, nor yet disbelieving in the virtues that will always remain such, and that are healthy and hearty; but as his jovial and sincere temperament gave him a thorough dislike of hypocrisy, the licence of the times allowed him to be plain-spoken to an extent which was perilous to his animal spirits. . . ."[13] *The Provok'd Wife*, for example, "more true than pleasant," was needed in Vanbrugh's day as a corrective of sottishness.

Macaulay's review of Hunt's edition struck hard once again at the issue of morality. Restoration comedy, "a disgrace to our language and our national character,"[14] is a systematic attempt to ridicule virtue and to approve vice. Especially pernicious, Macaulay argued, was the practice in Restoration comedy of associating vice with conjugal fidelity, and he offered Constant and Sir John Brute as illustrations of the ridiculed husband and the approved seducer. The review, unfortunately, is devoted almost exclusively to Wycherley and Congreve; therefore, the degree of guilt that Macaulay might have assigned to Vanbrugh can never be known. He defends Lord Foppington's contemptuous remarks on church attendance, however, as evidence of Vanbrugh's reverence. In doing so, he demonstrates that, had he undertaken to review Vanbrugh's work, he might have found it more difficult to fit into his own oversimplified estimation of manners comedy.

By the time the nineteenth century neared its end, Vanbrugh had begun to recover a little from fifty years of neglect. George Meredith alluded to him, to be sure, in his aphoristic and metaphoric "An Essay on Comedy" (1877); but he found Hoyden and the whole cast of Restoration comic characters as dead as last year's fashions. But, with the coming of W. C. Ward's two volume edition of the *Works* in 1893, a whole new chapter was opened in Vanbrugh criticism, one that is too large in its scope to be surveyed here. Ward's Introduction to the *Works* restored the balance that Macaulay had disturbed; for Ward asserted that the apparent licentiousness in Vanbrugh's plays had a satiric moral purpose despite the presence in *The Relapse* and in *The Provok'd Wife* of scenes that "transgress the bounds of decorum." After Ward's praise, Augustine Birrell praised Vanbrugh as a man who presented important ideas in striking images. In 1896, another edition was prepared for the popular Mermaid Series by A. E. H. Swaen; and, though it added nothing to Vanbrugh criticism, it represented a growing interest in the comic dramatist that began to gain momentum as the new century opened.

The most important event in the twentieth century life of Vanbrugh's reputation, however, was the publication in 1913 of John Palmer's *The Comedy of Manners*, a collection of uneven essays about the five great comic dramatists of the Restoration period—Etherege, Wycherley, Congreve, Vanbrugh, and Farquhar. By treating seventeenth century comedy as a dramatic and literary art that deserved to be taken seriously, Palmer opened the way for a veritable flood in the 1920's of articles, editions, and books about comedy in general and about the dramatist-architect's work in particular. Two of Palmer's statements, as a matter of fact, have served as starting points for virtually every critic who has since evaluated Vanbrugh's contribution to comic drama. "The English comedy of manners," he said, "began with Etherege; rose to perfection in Congreve; declined by easy stages with Vanbrugh and Farquhar; and was finally extinguished in Sheridan and Goldsmith." As to Vanbrugh's peculiar contribution to this process, Palmer states that "Adultery is no longer treated in the dry light of comedy. It is passionate; it takes to itself fine names. It is a comedy of heaving bosoms, and seductive phrase. Vanbrugh, in fact, killed the comedy of sex for the English theatre."[15]

A rather different charge—and one that serves as a starting point for the last paragraphs of this study of Vanbrugh's life and works—is Palmer's claim that the playwright was an inconsistent artist "who accepted the convention of Restoration comedy without being of the Restoration world." To Palmer, there is "a suspicion of uncertainty and unreality" when Vanbrugh deals with issues because he wished to invest his personages with one sort of character but was forced by Restoration comic conventions to invest them with another. "He hesitates between two kingdoms. Society was in revolution, and Vanbrugh belonged to the new period. But he accepted for his models a comedy based upon the old. His theatre no longer reflects the moral values of life. The connexion is broken, and confusion has ensued."[16]

One of the difficulties with such an estimate of Vanbrugh, as a playwright who put new wine in old skins, is Palmer's assumption that Congreve can serve as a touchstone for the treatment of comic materials in the late seventeenth century. If the stage history of comedies in the lifetime of Vanbrugh and Congreve is any measure, Congreve's treatment was not the most successful with audiences, whatever its literary merit; for Farquhar's two masterpieces and Dryden's *The Spanish Friar* outstripped in popularity any comedy by Congreve.[17] Even if we accept Congreve as the exemplar of Restoration comedy, there is no reason that Vanbrugh must be judged exclusively by his standards—as Palmer does. The comedy of wit and manners that "began with Etherege, rose to perfection in Congreve" was a narrowly limited type because it was created for an exclusive circle of courtiers and men of wit and because it was remote from the life and morality of England at large. Vanbrugh speaks to a much larger audience and to a much different one.

It is, frankly, rather odd to assume that, because Vanbrugh wrote when Congreve did, he was trying to write as Congreve did—and not succeeding. As a matter of fact, Vanbrugh's strongest points as a comic dramatist—his infinitely popular "humours" characters, his ability to create rapid stage movement and to enliven his scenes with farce, and his grotesque and detailed narrative and description—are not usually regarded as the prevailing characteristics of Restoration comedy. If some of his people do look and sound like characters in Etherege, Wycherley, and Congreve, it is not because Vanbrugh was imitating his predecessors but because all four playwrights lived in the same world of wits, fops, and fools, and because they caught glimpses of similar comic visions.

The two remaining points in Palmer's estimate are similarly weak or inaccurate—the "suspicion of uncertainty and unreality" in Vanbrugh's treatment of serious issues, and his failure to reflect "the moral values of life." The playwright was, if anything, too realistic in his treatment of social questions; he was so realistic, in fact, that in *The Relapse* he creates the antecedent of nineteenth century problem drama (with a comic subplot) rather than a true comedy. He is too concerned with the moral challenges of a more serious generation, with probing more deeply into human motivations and creating characters who trouble themselves with uncomic questions of right and wrong. It is true that he might have done more, but then so might Congreve. Palmer's speculation that Vanbrugh "might have founded a new school of English comedy in strict relation with the new social period"[18] is a piece of idle sophistry. His comedy *was* related to the period; and his brilliant adaptation, *The Confederacy*, offered as likely a model for a new middle class comic drama as anything to be found in the century. Moreover, Vanbrugh's comedies anticipated Farquhar and Goldsmith because he exploited a social world of citizens and servants, of country and city life, that had little in common with the fashionable folly of Pall Mall.

An accurate twentieth century estimate of the contribution of Sir John Vanbrugh to comic drama must recognize, in short, that neither he nor his contemporaries considered his works as transitional or as part of a comic decline. Like Dryden, Vanbrugh must have seen himself at the apex of a poetic pyramid, for he was writing successful plays that combined the best qualities of the comedy of the Age of Elizabeth and of the Restoration. In drama, as in architecture, Vanbrugh's genius was to enlarge, to take a narrow set of conventions and to expand them into something quite new. Just as his buildings—like Castle Howard, Blenheim, and Seaton Delaval—combined England's romantic past with her martial present by enclosing vaster spaces than was ever done before—his plays brought together the comedy of wit, the comedy of "humours," and the comedy of farce. Moreover, Vanbrugh added to these a new concern with moral issues and produced a drama that enlarged the English comic universe beyond any bounds previously known. In doing so, however, he risked the overall success of his original plays. By combining comic and serious actions, by realistically mixing good and evil, and by leaving a part of the issue unresolved, Vanbrugh made something new and troublesome in comedy, a re-creation in semicomic terms of a flesh and blood world that presents a more powerful challenge to the critical faculties of audience and reader than any previous English comedy.

Like Vanbrugh's predecessors in Restoration comedy, the playwright was primarily interested in making sense out of sex; but, unlike them, he turned most of his attention to the problems of married life. While his contemporaries praised him as a master of easy, laughing comedy and of familiar English dialogue, he is seen today as the playwright who added farcical action to Restoration comedy and who probed more deeply than his fellow dramatists had done into human motivations, creating characters who too often trouble themselves with uncomic questions of right and wrong. In doing so, Vanbrugh put on the stage a number of memorable people: intelligent, witty but flawed heroines, who pursue pleasure or money with more verve than the men who pursue them; and a set of infinitely popular "humours" characters—like Sir John Brute and Lord Foppington—the most coveted acting roles of the eighteenth century.

Notes and References

Chapter One

1. The Kneller portrait has been reproduced in David Piper, *Catalogue of Seventeenth-Century Portraits* (Cambridge, 1963); in Bernard Harris, *Sir John Vanbrugh* (London, 1967); in Laurence Whistler, *Sir John Vanbrugh, Architect and Dramatist, 1664–1726* (New York, 1939); in H. Avray Tipping and Christopher Hussey, *English Homes: The Work of Sir John Vanbrugh and his School, 1699–1736* (New York, 1928); and, an engraving from the portrait, in *The Complete Works of Sir John Vanbrugh*, vol. IV, *The Letters*, ed. by Bonamy Dobrée and Geoffrey Webb (Bloomsbury, 1928; reprinted New York, 1968) (References to this volume will subsequently be referred to as *Works*, followed by volume and page numbers, i.e., *Works*, IV, 1.) The second portrait may be found in Bonamy Dobrée, *Essays in Biography, 1680–1726* (London, 1925; reprinted Freeport, New York, 1967); and in John Palmer, *The Comedy of Manners* (London, 1913; reprinted New York, 1962). This portrait is attributed by Piper to Thomas Murray (ca. 1718).

The Richardson portrait may be seen in Dobrée, *Essays in Biography*, and in *Sir John Vanbrugh*, edited by W. C. Ward (London, 1893), vol. I.

2. Vanbrugh's letter to Jacob Tonson, October 25, 1725, in *Works*, IV, 170.

3. Throughout this chapter I am indebted for information about Vanbrugh's family and early life to a number of important lives and biographical notices. The earliest account is Vanbrugh's own sketch, furnished on the occasion of his claiming a family coat of arms. Next is information supplied by Peter Le Neve, his colleague in the College of Arms (*History of the College of Arms*), followed by Colley Cibber's *An Apology for the Life of Colley Cibber* (London, 1740), the fullest source of information about Vanbrugh's career in the theater.

Various early lives are summarized in David Erskine Baker's *Biographia Dramatica* (London, 1764, 1811). Leigh Hunt provided a biographical sketch in his edition of Wycherley, Congreve, Vanbrugh, and Farquhar (London, 1840), incorporating Issac Disraeli's material on Blenheim (*Curiosities of Literature*, 3 vols. [London, 1825]). Arthur Ashpitel, under

"Vanbrugh" in the *Encyclopaedia Britannica*, 8th ed. (1860), pp. 515–19, adds new information about his career as herald. W. C. Ward, in the introduction to his edition of Vanbrugh's works, makes use of material from parish registers in London and Chester. A. E. H. Swaen's Mermaid edition (London, 1896; reprinted London, 1949) contains much genealogical information. The *Dictionary of National Biography* article by Thomas Seccombe (1922) collects considerable primary material and provides a full bibliography. The introduction by Bonamy Dobrée to the *Works* is a graceful outline of Vanbrugh's career. The standard biography is Whistler's *Sir John Vanbrugh, Architect and Dramatist*. Whistler's *The Imagination of Vanbrugh and His Fellow Artists* (London, 1954) is the standard work on his architectural career; it includes twenty-three newly printed letters.

4. Large numbers of children in a family were not unusual. Lord Nottingham, for example, mentioned by Vanbrugh in a letter to Tonson, had thirty by his second wife (*Works*, IV, 256).

5. Whistler, *Sir John Vanbrugh*, p. 14, does not give his source for this interesting piece of information.

6. Quoted in part in Whistler, *ibid.*, pp. 17–19, but undated and with no indication of the location of the original.

7. Tong's *Life of Mr. Matthew Henry* (London, 1716), pp. 98–99, as quoted in Ward, p. xv.

8. *Works*, I, 11.

9. *Poems of Jonathan Swift*, edited by Harold Williams (Oxford, 1937), vol. I, 86.

10. The Seventh Earl of Huntingdon, Theophilus Hastings (1650–1701), was one of the peers who signed the order proclaiming James II on February 6, 1685. He became a Tory after he and his regiment were imprisoned for a time in 1688 for supposedly attempting to poison the Earl of Bath in order to seize his citadel for James II.

11. Both Barnard and Rosenberg reprint the letter (John Barnard, "Sir John Vanbrugh: Two Unpublished Letters," *Huntington Library Quarterly*, XXIX [1966], 347–52; Albert Rosenberg, "New Light on Vanbrugh," *Philological Quarterly*, XLV [July 1966], 603–13).

12. *Works*, IV, 135.

13. The letter, carefully annotated, is printed by Rosenberg.

14. Bevil Skelton (fl. 1661–1692) began his diplomatic career in 1674 when he was dispatched to Vienna. He was moved to Holland in 1685 and then to France after he failed to keep Monmouth from sailing for England.

15. Rosenberg, p. 605.

16. *Ibid.*

17. Daniel Finch, the Second Earl of Nottingham (1647–1730), was head of the War Department from 1688–1693; secretary of state for Queen Anne; and president of council under George I. His note is cited in Rosenberg, pp. 611–12.

18. Bishop Gilbert Burnet, *History of His Own Time* (Dublin, 1734), vol. II, p. 90.

Chapter Two

1. John Dennis, *The Critical Works of John Dennis*, edited by Edward Niles Hooker (Baltimore, 1939), vol. II, p. 277.

2. *Ibid.*, I, 293.

3. Jeremy Collier, *A Short View of the Immorality and Profaneness of the English Stage* (New York and London, 1972), p. 2.

4. Colley Cibber, *An Apology for the Life of Colley Cibber*, edited by B. R. S. Fone (Ann Arbor, Michigan, 1968), p. 120. Colley Cibber (1671–1757) began his acting career with the united companies in 1690.

5. Sir Thomas Skipwith (fl. 1695–1707) had bought a fairly large interest in Drury Lane from Sir William Davenant's son Alexander, but he long retained it quietly, content to allow Rich to exercise the patent. Christopher Rich (d. 1714) was originally an attorney, and he used this knowledge in the many lawsuits that grew out of his money-seeking management of Drury Lane.

6. Thomas Betterton had used the phrase in his petition to the Lord Chamberlain, December 1694; the bulk of the petition is reprinted in Allardyce Nicoll, *A History of English Drama from 1660–1900*, 4th ed. vol. I, *Restoration Drama* (Cambridge, 1961), pp. 368–70.

7. Samuel Pepys thought Betterton "the best Actor in the world" (*Diary*, edited by Henry B. Wheatley, 2 vols. [New York, 1964], November 4, 1661). Betterton (1635?–1710) had begun his acting career when he joined Davenant's company at Lincoln's Inn Fields in 1661, and he was with the company when it united with the king's players in 1682.

8. The Reply of the Patentees, December 10, 1694, cited in Nicoll, vol. I, p. 371.

9. Cibber, p. 121.

10. The date is conjectural; new plays frequently opened on a Saturday; Robert Jennens had written on Thursday, November 19, that Drury Lane was to produce a new play on November 21; Lady Morley saw *The Relapse* on November 25 (Leslie Hotson, *The Commonwealth and Restoration Stage* [Cambridge, Massachusetts, 1928; reprinted New York, 1962], p. 377); and the play was advertised December 26–29. Information of the play's date and the details of performance are found in *The London Stage*, pt. 1, edited by William Van Lennep (Carbondale, Illinois, 1965), p. 470. In his *Diary*, John Evelyn describes the week of November 15–23 as "very stormy weather, rain, and inundations."

11. Hugh Hunt, "Restoration Acting," in *Restoration Theatre*, edited by John Russell Brown and Bernard Harris (London, 1965), p. 183. Women had first appeared on the London stage shortly after the Restoration.

Samuel Pepys saw *The Beggar's Bush* on January 3, 1661, "the first time
that ever I saw women come upon the stage."
  12. Cibber, p. 127.
  13. *Ibid.*, p. 126.
  14. Alexander Pope, *The Dunciad*, edited by James Sutherland, 2nd ed.,
vol. V of The Twickenham Edition of the *Poems of Alexander Pope*, general
editor, John Butt (London and New Haven, 1953), p. 282n. Pope had
confused Lord Foppington with Sir Fopling Flutter.
  15. Cibber, pp. 122, 164. Hunt (p. 184) points out that acting throughout
the period was realistic in style. Pope spoke approvingly of Vanbrugh as one
of four English prose writers who would be authoritative as a writer of
familiar dialogue (Joseph Spence, *Observations, Anecdotes, and Characters
of Books and Men* [Oxford, 1966], vol. II, p. 170).
  16. Henri Misson, *M. Misson's Memoirs and Observations in His Travels
over England*, translated by John Ozell (French ed., 1698; English ed.
London, 1719), pp. 219–20.
  17. Charles Gildon, *The Lives and Characters of the English Dramatick
Poets* . . . (London, 1698), p. 145, as cited in Staring B. Wells, ed., *A
Comparison Between the Two Stages*, Princeton Studies in English, Vol.
XXVI (1702; reprinted Princeton and London, 1942), p. 139.
  18. Wells, pp. 20–21.
  19. *Ibid.*, p. 19: " 'Twas well for Durfey her late Majesty never saw it;
Gad if she had, People wou'd ha' said, it had first been the cause of her
Illness, and then of her Death; for 'tis a mortifying Piece o' my Word; Yes,
yes,—it was Damn'd."
  20. Leo Hughes, *A Century of English Farce* (Princeton, 1956), p. 126;
Irvin Ehrenpreis, *Mr. Swift and his Contemporaries*, vol. I of *Swift: The
Man, His Works, and the Age* (London, 1962), p. 232n.
  21. Charles Montagu (1661–1715) was made Earl of Halifax in 1714. His
efforts in 1692 as a lord of the treasury resulted in the Bank of England. He
was rewarded by being made chancellor of the exchequer, a post he held
until he was forced to resign in 1699.
  22. Cf. *The London Stage*, pt. 1, pp. xxxv–xxxvi and xliii–xliv for details.
  23. Wells, pp. 20–21.
  24. Dobrée, *Essays in Biography*, pp. 78–79.
  25. Hotson, pp. 307–308.
  26. *Works*, I, xiv.
  27. The Collier Controversy has been much discussed. The two fullest
surveys of it are to be found in Joseph Wood Krutch, *Comedy and Conscience after the Restoration* (New York, 1924; reprinted New York, 1949);
Sister Rose Anthony, *The Jeremy Collier Stage Controversy* (Milwaukee,
Wisconsin, 1937; reprinted New York, 1966).
  28. The facts of Collier's life (1650–1726) are found in Sister Rose Anthony's biographical sketch.

29. Quoted in D. Crane Taylor, *William Congreve* (1931; reprinted New York, 1963), p. 123.

30. Quoted in De Witt C. Croissant, *Studies in the Work of Colley Cibber*, Bulletin of the University of Kansas, Humanistic Studies, vol. I, no. 1 (Lawrence, 1912), 34n.

31. Krutch, p. 168–73.

32. John Genest, cited in Taylor, p. 123.

33. Cibber, p. 151.

34. Cf. Emmett Avery, "Dancing and Pantomime on the English Stage, 1670–1737," *Studies in Philology*, XXXI (July 1934), 417–52.

35. Quoted in Robert J. Allen, *The Clubs of Augustan London*, Harvard Studies in English, vol. VII (Cambridge, 1933), p. 40; *The London Stage*, pt. 1, p. 522, gives the date of Prior's letter as January 8. Allen's account of the club is the most complete to be had.

36. Allen, p. 233.

37. Introductory anecdotes prefixed to *The Letters and Works of Lady Mary Wortley Montagu*, edited by Moy Thomas (1893), vol. I, quoted in George Paston [E. M. Symonds], *Lady Mary Wortley Montagu and Her Times* (New York, 1907), p. 3.

38. John Oldmixon, *The History of England*, vol. III (1735), cited in Allen, pp. 40–41. Jacob Tonson (1656?–1736), a bookseller and publisher, was the secretary and leading spirit of the Kit-Cat Club. His house at Barn Elms had a special room set aside for the club, and, according to Pope, he got the Kit-Cat portraits from Kneller by flattery and presents of venison and wine.

39. Rosenberg, p. 611. Captain John Tidcombe (1642–1713) was an early member of the Kit-Cat Club and a friend of Joseph Addison.

40. Charles Montagu (1660–1722), who succeeded as Earl of Manchester in 1682, was a fellow Kit-Cat for whom Vanbrugh was to build Kimbolton Castle. The third Earl of Carlisle, Charles Howard (1674–1738), was a close friend of Vanbrugh, who designed Castle Howard for him. John Vaughn, Lord Carberry (1640–1713), had the additional distinction of being called by Pepys "one of the lewdest fellows of the age."

41. Charles E. Ward, ed., *The Letters of John Dryden* (Durham, North Carolina, 1942; reprint New York, 1965), p. 136.

42. G. B. Hill's note (in Johnson's *The Lives of the English Poets* [Oxford, 1905], vol. I, p. 389) calls attention to a notice in *The Post-Boy* for April 30 that Dryden "lies a dying."

43. Quoted in Allen, p. 233.

44. Leslie Stephen, "Dryden, John" In *The Dictionary of National Biography*, edited by Leslie Stephen and Sidney Lee, vol. VI (London, 1921–1922), p. 72. Dr. Samuel Garth (1661–1719), a strong Whig and amiable Kit-Cat, was knighted with Marlborough's sword on George I's accession.

45. *Works*, II, 151.

46. Quoted in Allen, p. 235.

47. Sir Christopher Wren (1632–1723) became surveyor-general of His Majesty's Works in 1661 and was an architect for the crown until 1714. Perhaps his most ambitious work was a master plan for the reconstruction of London after the Great Fire of 1666.

48. Cf. the detailed discussion of Vanbrugh's negotiations in acquiring the land in "The Haymarket Opera House," *Survey of London*, general editor F. H. W. Sheppard (London, 1960), vol. XXIX, ch. VIII, pp. 223–25; notes for the chapter are in vol. XXX, pp. 568–72.

49. Among them were the Duke of Newcastle, whose agreement is dated May 8, 1704, signed by Vanbrugh and witnessed by Congreve; Lord Carlisle, whose payment of the first twenty-five guineas is recorded in the Castle Howard accounts (Whistler, *The Imagination of Vanbrugh*, p. 39 and note); and the Earl of Bristol ("The Haymarket Opera House," p. 223).

50. Cibber, p. 172.

51. Allen, p. 237, attributes the May 5–12 account to Charles Leslie, a Tory journalist. The second journal is not named but is quoted by Donald C. Mullin ("The Queen's Theatre, Haymarket: Vanbrugh's Opera House," *Theatre Survey*, VIII [1967] 86), from Robert Wilkinson, *Londina Illustrata* (London, 1808), vol. II, n.p.

52. Percy Fitzgerald, *A New History of the English Stage* (London, 1882), vol. I, p. 238n. Charles Seymour (1662–1748), the sixth Duke of Somerset, aided William of Orange in 1688 and was a favorite of Anne.

53. William Walsh (1663–1708) was elected a member of Parliament on August 10, 1698, and was a longtime friend of Dryden and of Pope.

54. Montague Summers, ed., *The Complete Works of William Congreve* (London, 1924; reprint New York, 1964), vol. I, p. 76.

55. Cited in *ibid.*, pp. 57–58.

56. W. C. Ward, vol. I, pp. lii–liii.

57. Summers, vol. I, pp. 57–59.

58. John C. Hodges, "The Authorship of *Squire Trelooby*," *Review of English Studies*, IV (October 1928), 404–13.

59. John B. Shipley, "The Authorship of *The Cornish Squire*," *Philological Quarterly*, XLVII (April 1968), 145–56; Graham D. Harley, "*Squire Trelooby* and *The Cornish Squire*: A Reconsideration," *Philological Quarterly*, XLIX (October 1970), 520–29.

60. Printed in full in Whistler, *Sir John Vanbrugh*, p. 106.

61. The license is reproduced in Allardyce Nicoll, *A History of English Drama from 1660–1900*, 3rd ed., vol. II, *Early Eighteenth Century Drama* (Cambridge, 1952), p. 275.

62. Letter of November 20, 1713, *Works*, IV, 57.

63. Details of the production, marking the advent of opera in England, are found in *The London Stage*, pt. 2, vol. I, pp. lxxi–lxxii and 85 ff.

64. Taylor, p. 188.

65. Montague Summers, ed., *Roscius Anglicanus* (London, 1929; reprint New York, 1968), p. 48. John Downes (1662–1710) began to be a prompter at the time of the Restoration, having failed as an actor. From his prompting notes he wrote *Roscius Anglicanus*, a history of the plays given at the theaters with notes about each performance.

66. Emmett L. Avery, "The Capacity of the Queen's Theatre in the Haymarket," *Philological Quarterly*, XXXI (January 1952), 85–87; see also "The Haymarket Opera House," pp. 226–28, and Sheppard, ed., *Survey of London*, vol. XXX, plates 24–27, for a description and plans.

67. Cibber, p. 173.

68. The epilogue is attributed to Congreve in an undated work, "Prologues and Epilogues celebrated for their Poetical Merit" (Oxford), cited in W. J. Lawrence, "The Early Years of the First English Opera House," *The Musical Quarterly*, vol. VII (January 1921), 108.

69. *Private Correspondence of Sara Duchess of Marlborough*, cited in W. C. Ward, vol. I, pp. lv–lvi. Arthur Mainwaring (1668–1712) had given up law after the death of his father in 1693 to devote himself to politics and society by placing his pen and wit at the service of the government. By 1705 he was appointed auditor of imprests and in 1706 he was elected a member of Parliament.

70. Whistler, *Sir John Vanbrugh*, p. 113.

71. The anonymous author of "Hell upon Earth," written about this time, complained of *The Provok'd Wife* and other comedies, "The more they have been expos'd by Mr. *Collier* and others, the more they seem to be admir'd!" W. C. Ward, vol. I, p. xxxii.

72. Lawrence, pp. 110–11.

73. See R. H. Barker's excellent account of the complicated proceedings that followed, *Mr. Cibber of Drury Lane* (New York and Oxford, 1939), pp. 62–68.

74. Owen Mac Swiney (d. 1754) was an Irish playwright who had come to London to manage Queen's. His management of the theater left him bankrupt and compelled him to take refuge abroad.

75. Summers, *Congreve*, vol. I, p. 80.

76. Nicoll (3rd ed.), vol. II, p. 282.

77. Cibber, pp. 199–200. Colonel Henry Brett (d. 1724) was a close friend of Cibber and a member of Addison's circle. In 1700 he married the divorced Countess of Macclesfield (alleged by Richard Savage to have been Savage's mother).

78. Mullin, p. 92.

79. Ronald Kern, "Documents Relating to Company Management, 1705–1711," *Theatre Notebook*, XIV (Winter 1959), 64.

80. The letter is reprinted in my article "Vanbrugh: Additions to the Correspondence," *Philological Quarterly*, LIII (January 1974), 136–37.

81. The document, taken from a transcript, is printed in Philip Olleson,

"Vanbrugh and Opera at the Queen's Theatre, Haymarket," *Theatre Notebook*, XXVI (Spring 1972), 98.

82. *Ibid*. For correct capitalization and the like, I have relied on the original, manuscript no. 18 in the Carl and Lily Pforzheimer Foundation's collection.

83. The letter is reprinted in Rosenberg, pp: 606–07, and in Barnard, pp. 349–51.

84. Palmer, p. 208.

85. Attacks upon opera increased in intensity from the opening of Queen's in 1705. Thomas Rymer had charged opera with a "conspiracy against nature and good sense" (*Short View of Tragedy*, 1693); John Dennis damned it as "a diversion of more pernicious consequence than the most licentious play" (*An Essay on the Opera's*, 1706) and criticized the "extravagant encouragement" given it (*Essay upon Publick Spirit*, 1711); Charles Gildon blamed the "people of figure" who conspired to ruin drama "by prodigal subscriptions for squeaking Italians and cap'ring Monsieurs" (*The Life of Thomas Betterton*, 1710).

Most of the many complaints were against the emphasis upon opera's spectacle and its effeminacy. Addison and Steele attacked it on these two points in *The Spectator*, as did Pope in a number of places (see my article "Pope's Critical Views of the London Stage," *Restoration and 18th Century Theatre Research*, III [May 1964], 25–37); and Swift complained in the *Intelligencer* (no. 3, 1728) about Italian nonsense and effeminacy on stage. Not until the remarkable success of John Gay's *The Beggar's Opera* did the criticism abate.

86. Letter to Manchester, July 27, 1708, *Works*, IV, 24.

87. The Vanbrugh family maintained a leasehold interest in the Haymarket property until July 24, 1789, when Sir John's nephew Edward sold it to Giovanni Gallini and R. B. O'Reilly. The theater itself had burned to the ground on June 17, 1789.

88. Letter to Tonson, June 18, 1722, *Works*, IV, 146.

89. Thomas Davies, *Dramatic Miscellanies*, III (London, 1784), p. 261.

90. Anonymous, *Daily Journal*, January 12, 1728; Richard Cumberland cites George Bubb Dodington as confirmation of Cibber's words ("Critique on *The Provok'd Husband*," *The British Drama*, VI [London, 1817], xx).

Chapter Three

1. According to Cibber, p. 121, *The Relapse* was in the hands of the patentees at the beginning of April, and they accepted it for the following season.

2. Cibber's entertaining account of the success of *Love's Last Shift* is found in *Apology*, pp. 118–20. His acting was, of course, sufficiently competent throughout his long career to make him a stage favorite in many roles, although he had numerous detractors. Sir Richard Steele, writing a quarter

of a century later in *The Theatre*, praised Cibber's thespian genius and explained the criticism as the result of Cibber's so frequently acting contemptible parts (*Richard Steele's The Theatre: 1720*, edited by John Loftis [Oxford, 1962], pp. 28–29).

3. Dobrée, "The Architect of Blenheim," *Essays in Biography*, pp. 67–68. See also Dobrée's remarks, *Works*, I, xiv; Dobrée follows David Erskine Baker, Issac Reed, and Stephen Jones, *Biographia Dramatica* (London, 1811; reprinted Graz, Austria, 1967), III, 200. Baker, whose remarks date from 1764, seems to have been the first to argue that Vanbrugh's *Relapse* is a criticism of the faulty morality of Cibber's play.

4. Paul Mueschke and Jeannette Fleisher, "A Re-evaluation of Vanbrugh," *Publications of the Modern Language Association*, XLIX (September 1934), 850–51. Many students of Restoration drama have followed Baker's lead: L. R. N. Ashley, *Colley Cibber*, (New York, 1965), pp. 43–44; Marianne Kunerth Mayo, "John Vanbrugh's *The Relapse*: A Study of its Meaning" (Ph.D. dissertation, University of Florida, 1968), pp. 7, 24, and *passim*; Frank M. Patterson, "The Achievement of Sir John Vanbrugh" (Ph.D. dissertation, University of Iowa, 1966), pp. 1–2 and 54, speaks ironically of Loveless's beginning as a rake and ending as "a model of moral propriety, having been converted by that paragon of constancy, Amanda, his wife"; Gerald Berkowitz, "The Plays of Sir John Vanbrugh and the Comedy of the Late Seventeenth Century" (Ph.D. dissertation, Indiana University, 1969), pp. 132, 182, observes that Vanbrugh deliberately reacted against the sentimentality of Cibber's play and that "Vanbrugh's Worthy is not so easily won over as Cibber's Loveless by the magic of country virtue"; C. R. Kropf, "*The Relapse* and the Sentimental Mask," *Journal of Narrative Technique*, I (September 1971), 193–99, argues that in the Loveless-Amanda plot Vanbrugh is illustrating "the futility of sentimental morality."

5. Cibber, *Love's Last Shift: or, The Fool in Fashion*, vol. III of *The Dramatick Works of Colley Cibber, Esq.* (London 1736), p. 40. This five volume edition has been omitted from the bibliographies of Barker, and those of Ashley (*Colley Cibber;* and "Colley Cibber: A Bibliography," *Restoration and 18th Century Theatre Research*, VI [May 1967], pp. 14–27 and [November 1967] pp. 51–57) Croissant includes it but with the date 1636. It is valuable as the last collected edition published in Cibber's lifetime.

6. Cibber, *Dramatick Works*, III, 49.

7. *Ibid.*, p. 85.

8. *Ibid.*, p. 94

9. *Ibid.*, p. 14.

10. *Ibid.*, p. 67.

11. *Ibid.*, p. 90.

12. *Ibid.*, p. 86.

13. Louis Kronenberger says it well: "Loveless has not been so much

reformed as bought, Amanda regaining him only when he learns she is an heiress" (*The Thread of Laughter* [New York, 1952], p. 150).

14. *Works*, I, 210–11. The italics in the passage are mine.

15. Croissant, p. 45.

16. B. R. S. Fone, *"Love's Last Shift* and Sentimental Comedy II," *Restoration and 18th Century Theatre Research*, IX (May 1970), 12–13.

17. Cf. Paul E. Parnell, "Equivocation in Cibber's *Love's Last Shift*," *Studies in Philology*, XLVII (January 1960), 519–34, who points out that Cibber wrote for a combined audience of middle class patrons and admirers of Restoration wit, hence the mixture.

18. Ashley, *Colley Cibber*, p. 40; Fone demonstrates (pp. 16–18) that the new morality is to be found in the play from beginning to end, with comedy and bawdry continually subordinated to preachment and morality.

19. Dougald MacMillan, "The Text of *Love's Last Shift*," *Modern Language Notes*, XLVI (1931), 518–19.

20. Elmer Stoll, "The 'Real Society' in Restoration Comedy: Hymeneal Pretenses," *Modern Language Notes*, XLVIII (March 1943), 176.

21. G. S. Alleman, *Matrimonial Law and the Materials of Restoration Comedy* (Wallingford, Pennsylvania, 1942), pp. 44, 53, 70.

22. Bonamy Dobrée, *Restoration Comedy* (Oxford, 1924), p. 152.

23. Montague Summers calls attention to the passage in *The Restoration Theatre* (London, 1934; reprinted New York, 1964), p. 104.

24. Mayo (pp. 63–66) believes that Loveless's language suggests Stoicism—although Epicurean elements are present—but that he lacks true Stoic strength.

25. A useful discussion of the influence of Hobbes upon Restoration comedy is that by Samuel Abba Weiss, "Hobbism and Restoration Comedy" (Ph.D. dissertation, Columbia University, 1953). Especially relevant to Loveless are pp. 10–12, 44, 61–62.

26. William Congreve, "Concerning Humour in Comedy (1695)," in *Critical Essays of the Seventeenth Century*, edited by J. E. Spingarn, vol. III (Oxford, 1909; reprinted Bloomington, Indiana, 1957), p. 250; Heartfree in *The Provok'd Wife* describes women as cold by nature (Act II, scene i).

27. *John Milton: Complete Poems and Major Prose*, ed. by Merrit Y. Hughes (New York, 1957), p. 728.

28. For a fuller discussion of Amanda's Christian faith, see Mayo, pp. 67–70, 113–26.

29. Mueschke and Fleisher, p. 888.

30. John Harrington Smith calls the conversion "yet another triumph of female virtue over male libertinism" (*The Gay Couple* [Cambridge, 1948], p. 173). Three useful articles by David S. Berkeley treat the conversion theme: "The Penitent Rake in Restoration Comedy," *Modern Philology*, XLIX (May 1952), 223–33; "The Art of 'Whining' Love," *Studies in Philol-*

ogy, LII (July 1955), 478–96; "Présiosité and the Restoration Comedy of Manners," *Huntington Library Quarterly*, XVIII (February 1955), 109–28. In the last named essay, Berkeley calls it "an article of *précieuse* faith . . . that ladies of beauty and goodness could instantly convert rakes and villains to a state of unspotted virtue" (p. 120).

31. In a recent article, Pieter Jan Van Niel argues that *The Relapse* is instead a play that demonstrates the powers of darkness ("*The Relapse*— Into Death and Damnation," *Educational Theatre Journal*, XXI [October 1969], 318–32).

32. Mueschke and Fleisher (p. 855) argue that in the scene "Vanbrugh derives as much fun as did his audience, or Wycherley in Horner's china scene. . . ."

33. William Hazlitt, "Lecture IV," in *Lectures on the English Comic Writers* (London, 1819; reprinted New York n.d.), p. 113.

34. W. Matthews notes that Foppington's affected speech is not unique to him ("Two Notes upon Seventeenth Century Pronunciation," *Journal of English and Germanic Philology*, XXXII [July 1933], 296–98). There have been attempts to assign sources beyond Cibber for Foppington's character: Dobreé (*Restoration Comedy*, p. 27) suggests the famous Beau Fielding as a model, even to the duel scene; and John Wilcox, *The Relation of Molière to Restoration Comedy* (New York and Oxford, 1938), p. 168, suggests M. Jourdain as a model, noting in particular Act II, scene 5 of *Le Bourgeois Gentilhomme* as a source for Lord Foppington's exchange with his shoemaker.

35. Cibber, *Dramatick Works*, III, 40.

36. Congreve, "Concerning Humour in Comedy," in *Critical Essays of the Seventeenth Century* vol. III, 246.

37. Weiss (p. 45) finds Foppington's description of his day to be the best statement on pleasure in Restoration comedy, and traces this pleasure philosophy in part to Hobbes.

38. Because Lord Foppington is essentially middle class, he is not really—as David S. Berkeley claims—an exception to the rule that the peerage is not to be ridiculed on stage ("Some Notes on Probability in Restoration Drama," *Notes and Queries*, CC [1955], 237–39, 342–44, 432).

39. Lytton Strachey, *Characters and Commentaries* (New York, 1933), p. 161.

40. Patterson, "The Achievement of Sir John Vanbrugh," passim; H. J. Habakkuk, "Marriage Settlements in the Eighteenth Century," *Transactions of the Royal Historical Society*, 4th series, XXXII (1950), 15–30.

41. The subject has been only briefly treated. Montague Summers (*The Playhouse of Pepys* [London, 1935; reprint New York, 1964], p. 294) has noted the comedies by Dilke and Granville; Patterson, "The Achievement of Sir John Vanbrugh" (p. 65), points to the Otway parallel; and G. Wilson

Knight (*The Golden Labyrinth* [London, 1962], p. 138), after noticing Otway and Behn, points to Southerne's *Sir Anthony Love or The Rambling Lady* (1691), where the treatment of homosexuality is extensive.

42. Hazlitt, p. 117. Vanbrugh may have borrowed the name Hoyden from Wycherley's *The Plain Dealer* (1676), where Olivia describes a Mrs. Hoyden as "familiar as a duck."

43. Pope to Henry Cromwell, November 25, 1710; George Sherburn, ed., *The Correspondence of Alexander Pope* (Oxford, 1956), vol. I, 106.

44. Blaise Pascal, *Pascal's Pensées*, edited by H. F. Stewart (New York, 1950), p. 70 (my translation).

45. Dennis, "The Person of Quality's Answer . . . (1704)," in *Works*, p. 310; T. S. Eliot, "A Dialogue on Dramatic Poetry" (1928), in *Selected Essays*, 2nd ed. (New York, 1950), pp. 33, 40.

Chapter Four

1. Mueschke and Fleisher, pp. 877–78.

2. *The Dramatic Works of Sir George Etherege*, edited by H. F. B. Brett-Smith (Oxford, 1927), vol. II, pp. 94–95.

3. Antony Coleman, "Sir John Brute on the Eighteenth Century Stage," *Restoration and 18th Century Theatre Research*, VIII (November 1969), 41–46; cf. Kalman A. Burnim, *David Garrick: Director* (Pittsburgh, 1961), pp. 176–79.

4. Hazlitt, p. 118.

5. The exact date of the revisions has not been finally determined. Professor Curt Zimansky, editor of the most recent edition of *The Provoked Wife*, argues for 1725 on the basis of Colley Cibber's statement in the *Apology* (pp. 308–09) that in 1725 the company was called upon to revive the play and that Vanbrugh "was prevail'd upon, to substitute a new-written Scene." But Cibber's memory is notorious for its inaccuracy in matters of detail, and the statement in the *Apology* is at least ambiguous, for "new-written" can mean the scenes were composed at any time after the initial performance in 1697. Dobrée (*Works*, I, 186) prefers the 1705 date because the 1706 revival was advertised as "with alterations" and because John Genest says the substitute scenes were written for the 1706 performance. Alwin Thaler, who agrees with Dobrée, suggests that the idea for the change from a parson's gown to a woman's dress occurred to Vanbrugh when he was revising *Squire Trelooby* for its revival a week after the *Provok'd Wife* revival in January 1706. In Act III of *Squire Trelooby*, the squire disguises himself as a woman and is arrested by a constable and a watchman, just as Brute does in the revised scene (Alwin Thaler, "Sir John Vanbrugh: *The Provok'd Wife*—Critical Essay," in *Dryden and His Contemporaries*, vol. IV of *Representative English Comedies*, edited by Charles Mills Gayley and Alwin Thaler [New York, 1936], pp. 422–23); Frank M. Patterson argues that, regardless of which date is right for the revisions, the *original* version

continued to be played into the early 1730's ("The Revised Scenes of *The Provok'd Wife," English Language Notes*, IV [September 1966], 19–23).

6. An excellent examination of the place of "whining love" and *préciosité* generally in Restoration comedy is that by Berkeley, "Préciosité and the Restoration Comedy of Manners," pp. 109–28; see also his article "The Art of 'Whining' Love," pp. 478–96.

7. Richard Cumberland is the first to suggest that the match between Heartfree and Bellinda "violates . . . the consistency of Heartfree's character" ("Critique on *The Provok'd Wife*," p. ix); but it appears from Heartfree's first meeting with Lady Fancyfull that he is already very nearly in love and could fall for the first woman who had beauty but lacked affectation.

8. Augustine Birrell, "Sir John Vanbrugh (1894)," in *The Collected Essays and Addresses 1880–1920* (New York, 1894; reprint Freeport, New York, 1968), p. 109.

9. Hazlitt, p. 113.

10. Cibber, *Dramatick Works*, p. 85.

11. Collier, pp. 140–41.

12. Weiss (p. 58) considers her to be the spokesman in the play for Hobbesian libertine ethics.

13. Mueschke and Fleisher, pp. 873–79.

14. Alleman, p. 107.

15. Montagu, *The Complete Letters of Lady Mary Wortley Montagu*, edited by Robert Halsband (Oxford, 1965), vol. I, 201. *Works*, IV, 111–12.

Chapter Five

1. Editions consulted: Édme Boursault, *Théâtre de Feu Boursault*, vol. III (Paris, 1725); Florent Dancourt, *Les Oeuvres de Théâtre de M. Dancourt*, vol. I (Paris, 1760); A. R. Waller, ed., *The Works of Francis Beaumont and John Fletcher*, vol. V (Cambridge, 1907); A. René Lesage, *Oeuvres*, vol. XI (Paris, 1828); A. R. Waller, ed., *The Plays of Molière in French with an English Translation and Notes*, vol. I, (Edinburgh, 1907).

2. Despite Dobrée (*Works*, II, 3), there is not even the flimsiest connection between *Aesop II* and Boursault's sequel *Ésope à la Cour;* Patterson, whose chapter on the translated plays is thorough and accurate, dismisses any relationship on internal grounds ("The Achievement of Sir John Vanbrugh," p. 88). But it is necessary only to note that Boursault's *Ésope à la Cour*, which belongs to the year 1701, could have had no influence on *Aesop II*, staged four years *earlier*, in March 1697 (Sidney D. Braun, ed., *Dictionary of French Literature* [Greenwich, Connecticut, 1964], p. 52; and Henry Carrington Lancaster, *A History of French Dramatic Literature in the Seventeenth Century*, part V [Baltimore, 1942; reprint New York, 1966], p. 124).

3. Wells, pp. 95–96.

4. Hazlitt, p. 116.
5. W. C. Ward, vol. I, p. liv.
6. Berkowitz, pp. 71–72.
7. Lancaster, vol. I, 109–10.
8. John Downes. *Roscius Anglicanus* (London, 1708; reprinted Los Angeles, 1969), p. 49. Wilcox, pp. 173–74.

Chapter Six

1. Dobrée, in *Works*, III, 179.
2. Cumberland, p. xx.
3. See Marilyn Klawiter, "Colley Cibber as Comic Playwright" (Ph.D. dissertation, University of Chicago, 1971), p. 236: "To one more familiar with Cibber's plays than with his stage personality, it is difficult to understand the confusion of the original audience as to which part of the play was Cibber's."
4. Cibber, *Apology*, p. 320.
5. A thorough survey of the stage career of Vanbrugh's plays is found in Patterson, "The Achievement of Sir John Vanbrugh," pp. 133–82, 218.
6. Gildon, cited in Wells, p. 142.
7. Giles Jacob, *The Poetical Register* (London, 1719), vol. I, p. 262.
8. Spence, vol. II, pp. 170, 206–07.
9. Cibber, *Apology* p. 122.
10. Charles Lamb, "On the Artificial Comedy of the Last Century," *The Collected Essays of Charles Lamb* (London, 1929), vol. I, p. 165.
11. *Ibid.*, p. 168.
12. Hazlitt, pp. 127–28.
13. Leigh Hunt, "John Vanbrugh," in *Sir John Vanbrugh*, ed. A. E. H. Swain [sic] (London, 1949), p. 34.
14. Thomas Babington Macaulay, "Leigh Hunt: Comic Dramatists of the Restoration," in *The Miscellaneous Works of Lord Macaulay*, ed. Lady Trevelyan, vol. V, p. 114 (Philadelphia, n. d.).
15. Palmer, pp. 2, 224.
16. *Ibid.*, p. 236.
17. A survey of performances in the first three decades of the eighteenth century shows Farquhar's *The Recruiting Officer* in first place with 164 performances, followed by *The Beaux' Stratagem* (135) and Dryden's *The Spanish Friar* (129). Then come *Love for Love*, Howard's *The Committee*, Cibber's *Love Makes a Man*, *The Old Batchelor*, Centlivre's *The Busy Body*, Cibber's *The Careless Husband*, Behn's *The Rover*, and Vanbrugh's *The Relapse* (*The London Stage*, Part 1).
18. Palmer, p. 236.

Selected Bibliography

PRIMARY SOURCES

1. First and Modern Editions of Individual Plays

The Relapse; or, Virtue in Danger: being the sequel of The fool in fashion, a comedy. London: Printed for Samuel Briscoe, 1697.

The Relapse. Edited by Curt A. Zimansky. Lincoln, Nebraska: University of Nebraska Press, 1970.

The Relapse. Edited by Bernard Harris. London: Ernest Benn, 1971.

Aesop. A Comedy. As it is acted at the Theatre-Royal in Drury-Lane. London: T. Bennet, 1697.

Aesop. Part the second. London: T. Bennet, 1697.

The Provok'd Wife: a comedy, as it is acted at the New theatre, in Little Lincoln's-Inn-Fields. London: Printed by J. O. for R. Wellington and Sam. Briscoe, 1697.

The Provoked Wife. Edited by Curt A. Zimansky. Lincoln, Nebraska: University of Nebraska Press, 1969.

The Pilgrim, a comedy: as it is acted at the Theatre-Royal in Drury-Lane. London: Printed for Benjamin Tooke, 1700.

The False Friend, a comedy. As it is acted at the Theatre-Royal in Drury-Lane. London: Printed for Jacob Tonson, 1702.

Squire Trelooby. Acted at the Subscription Musick at the Theatre Royal in Lincoln's-Inn-Fields. London: 1704. Perhaps the work of Vanbrugh, Congreve, and Walsh. A similar version of the play, attributed to Vanbrugh and his friends, was published by James Ralph as *The Cornish Squire*. London: Printed for J. Watts, 1734.

The Confederacy. A comedy. As it is acted at the Queen's theatre in the Hay-market. London: J. Tonson, 1705.

The Mistake. A comedy. As it is acted at the Queen's theatre in the Hay-Market. London: J. Tonson, 1706.

The Country House. A farce, etc. London: W. Meares, Jonas Browne, 1715.

The Provok'd Husband; or, A Journey to London. A comedy, as it is acted at the Theatre-royal, by His Majesty's servants. Written by the late Sir John Vanbrugh, and Mr. Cibber. . . . London: Printed for J. Watts, 1728. Includes *A Journey to London, Being part of a comedy written by*

*the late Sir John Vanbrugh, knt. and printed after his own copy: which
(since his decease) has been made an intire play, by Mr. Cibber. And
called, The provok'd husband,* &c.
The Provoked Husband. Edited by Peter Dixon. Lincoln, Nebraska: University of Nebraska Press, 1973.
2. Nondramatic Works
"A Short Vindication of *The Relapse* and *The Provok'd Wife*, from Immorality and Prophaneness." By the author. London: Walwyn, 1698.
"The Justification of What he Depos'd," etc. London: 1721.
3. Collected Editions
Plays. 2 vols. London: J. D. for J. Tonson & M. Wellington, 1719. First collected edition.
Works. 2 vols. London: n.p., 1730.
Plays. 2 vols. London: J. Tonson, 1734.
Plays. 2 vols. London: W. Feales et al., 1735.
Plays. 2 vols. London: n.p., 1739.
Plays. 2 vols. London: C. Hitch and L. Hawes, 1759.
Plays. 2 vols. London: J. Rivington et al., 1776.
The Dramatic Works of Wycherley, Congreve, Vanbrugh, and Farquhar. Edited by Leigh Hunt. London: E. Moxon, 1840. Followed by several reprints.
Sir John Vanbrugh. Edited by W. C. Ward. 2 vols. London: Lawrence & Bullen, 1893.
Sir John Vanbrugh. Edited by A. E. H. Swaen. London: T. F. Unwin, 1896; reprinted London: Ernest Benn Limited, 1949.
The Complete Works of Sir John Vanbrugh. Edited by Bonamy Dobrée and Geoffrey Webb. 4 vols. Bloomsbury: The Nonesuch Press, 1927–1928; reprinted New York: AMS Press, 1968. The standard edition of the plays, miscellaneous prose, and letters. The plays form vols. I–III; vol. IV contains the letters.

SECONDARY SOURCES

1. Books
ALLEMAN, GELLERT SPENCER. *Matrimonial Law and the Materials of Restoration Comedy.* Wallingford, Pennsylvania: The University of Pennsylvania Press, 1942. Definitive discussion; surveys 241 Restoration plays.
ALLEN, ROBERT J. *The Clubs of Augustan London.* Harvard Studies in English, vol. VII. Cambridge, Massachusetts: Harvard University Press, 1933. Includes an excellent survey of the Kit-Cat Club.
ANTHONY, SISTER ROSE. *The Jeremy Collier Stage Controversy, 1698–1726.* Milwaukee, Wisconsin: Marquette University Press, 1937; reprinted New York: Benjamin Blom, 1966. Study of controversy

aroused by Collier's *Short View*. Includes a life of Collier; summarizes the various charges and countercharges.

ASHLEY, LEONARD R. N. *Colley Cibber*. New York: Twayne Publishers, 1965. Standard critical biography of the man whose *Love's Last Shift* inspired Vanbrugh to write *The Relapse* and whose rewriting of *A Journey to London* brought Vanbrugh's writing career to a posthumous end.

BARKER, RICHARD HINDRY. *Mr. Cibber of Drury Lane*. Columbia University Studies in English and Comparative Literature, no. 143. New York: Columbia University Press, and Oxford: Oxford University Press, 1939. Scholarly, readable life of Vanbrugh's friend and "reviser"; largely replaced by Ashley's study.

BATESON, F. W. *English Comic Drama, 1700–1750*. Oxford: Clarendon Press, 1929; reprinted New York: Russell & Russell, 1963. Standard survey of the drama that succeeded Vanbrugh.

BERNBAUM, ERNEST. *The Drama of Sensibility*. Boston: Ginn & Co., 1915. Still a sound study of sentimental comedy.

BINGHAM, MADELEINE. *Masks and Façades; Sir John Vanbrugh, the Man in His Setting*. London: George Allen and Unwin, Ltd., 1974. A rewriting of Laurence Whistler's *Sir John Vanbrugh* (1939) with little new material added. Bingham neglects much of the research of the past forty years and offers little documentation for her generalizations.

CHETWOOD, WILLIAM RUFUS. *A General History of the Stage*. London: W. Owen, 1749. Full of anecdotes and gossip relating to Drury Lane, where Chetwood was prompter for twenty years.

CIBBER, COLLEY. *An Apology for the Life of Colley Cibber*. Ed. B. R. S. Fone. Ann Arbor: The University of Michigan Press, 1968. The text of the first edition (London, 1740). Contains many Vanbrugh references, including the best eighteenth century estimate of his work.

COLLIER, JEREMY. *A Short View of the Immorality and Profaneness of the English Stage*. London: S. Keble et al., 1698; reprinted New York and London: Garland Publishing, 1972. Restoration comedy's most formidable antagonist; urges comedy as an instrument "to recommend Virtue, and discountenance Vice."

CROISSANT, DE WITT C. *Studies in the Work of Colley Cibber*. Bulletin of the University of Kansas, Humanistic Studies, vol. I, no. 1 (Lawrence, Kansas, 1912).

DAMETZ, MAX. *Vanbrughs Leben und Werke*. Wien und Liepzig: Wilhelm Braumuller, 1898. Surveys his life, original comedies, and translations. Assigns his work to the tradition of Molière rather than Boileau.

DOBRÉE, BONAMY. *Essays in Biography, 1680–1726*. London: Oxford University Press, 1925; reprinted Freeport, New York: Books for Libraries Press, 1967. The monograph on Vanbrugh is perceptive and

sympathetic but is given over almost entirely to the Blenheim con-
troversy.
————. *Restoration Comedy, 1660–1720*. Oxford: Clarendon Press, 1924.
Still a standard book on the subject. The essay on Vanbrugh praises his
originality in adding Elizabethan life to Restoration comedy.
HARRIS, BERNARD. *Sir John Vanbrugh*. London: Longmans, Green, 1967.
Urbane monograph, with a useful bibliography.
KRUTCH, JOSEPH WOOD. *Comedy and Conscience after the Restoration*.
New York: Columbia University Press, 1924; reprinted 1961. The Col-
lier controversy and its relationship to the society of the Restoration
and the emergence of sentimental comedy.
The London Stage, 1660–1800. 5 pts. in 11 vols. Carbondale: Southern
Illinois University Press, 1960–1968. Edited by various hands; an indis-
pensable record of Restoration and eighteenth century dramatic
performances.
MUIR, KENNETH. *The Comedy of Manners*. London: Hutchinson, 1970.
Includes an essay on Vanbrugh: his dialogue is less witty and his plots
less original than those of Wycherley, Congreve, and Farquhar.
NICOLL, ALLARDYCE. *A History of English Drama, 1660–1900*. 6 vols.
London: Cambridge University Press, 1952–1959. Vol. 1 covers Restoration drama; vol. II early eighteenth century drama. Much revised
since the appearance in 1923 of the first volume in the series, the work
is still an authoritative review of stage conditions.
PALMER, JOHN. *The Comedy of Manners*. London: G. Bell and Sons, Ltd.,
1913; reprinted New York: Russell and Russell, 1962. Pioneer study of
Restoration comedy; concludes that Vanbrugh "killed the comedy of
sex for the English theatre" (p. 224).
PERRY, HENRY TEN EYCK. *The Comic Spirit in Restoration Drama: Studies
in the Comedy of Etherege, Wycherley, Congreve, Vanbrugh, and
Farquhar*. New Haven: Yale University Press, 1925. Vanbrugh com-
promised with the public taste for sentimentality; and "his attempts to
probe the deep emotions of mankind are faltering and pathetic"
(p. 106).
SCHNEIDER, BEN ROSS, JR. *The Ethos of Restoration Comedy*. Urbana,
Chicago, London: University of Illinois Press, 1971. Surveys the
characters in eighty-three important comedies (including four by Vanbrugh), and concludes that the purpose of Restoration comedy was "to
mirror society in such a way as to criticize it" (p. 14).
SPRAGUE, ARTHUR C. *Beaumont and Fletcher on the Restoration Stage*.
Cambridge, Massachusetts: Harvard University Press, 1926. Gives the
stage history of Vanbrugh's *The Pilgrim*.
STRATMAN, CARL J., DAVID G. SPENCER, and MARY ELIZABETH DEVINE,
eds. *Restoration and Eighteenth Century Theatre Research: A Biblio-
graphical Guide 1900–1968*. Carbondale and Edwardsville: Southern

Illinois University Press, and London and Amsterdam: Feffer & Si-
mons, Inc., 1971. Definitive bibliography of twentieth century studies
in Restoration drama. Annotated.

SUMMERS, MONTAGUE. *A Bibliography of Restoration Drama*. London:
Fortune Press, [1935]. Includes a nearly complete listing of Vanbrugh's
individually published plays and collected works.

WELLS, STARING B. ed. *A Comparison Between the Two Stages*. Princeton,
New Jersey: Princeton Studies in English, Vol. XXVI, Princeton University Press, and London: Humphrey Milford, Oxford University
Press, 1942. Provides contemporary reactions to some of Vanbrugh's
plays, especially *The False Friend*.

WHISTLER, LAURENCE. *The Imagination of Vanbrugh and His Fellow Artists*. London: B. T. Batsford, and Toronto: Clarke, Irwin, 1954. Standard for Vanbrugh's architectural career. Includes a number of new
letters.

———. *Sir John Vanbrugh, Architect and Dramatist, 1664–1726*. New
York: Macmillan, 1939. Standard biography; sympathetic and full but
florid in style. Lacks footnotes and scholarly bibliography but includes
sixteen well-chosen illustrations.

WILCOX, JOHN. *The Relation of Molière to Restoration Comedy*. New York:
Columbia University Press, and Oxford: Oxford University Press,
1938. Vanbrugh's original plays show no trace of Molière's influence;
The Mistake is the first good acting translation of *Le Depit Amoureux*.

2. Theses and Dissertations

BERKOWITZ, GERALD. "The Plays of Sir John Vanbrugh and the Comedy of
the Late Seventeenth Century." Ph.D dissertation, Indiana University, 1969. Argues that Vanbrugh expands the comic world by introducing a new moral standard and by freeing comic drama from the conventions of Restoration comedy.

FAULKNER, THOMAS C. "Sir John Vanbrugh's Sympathetic Approach to
Comedy." Master's thesis, Miami University, 1964.

HARLEY, GRAHAM D. "Sir John Vanbrugh: A Critical and Historical
Study." Ph.D. dissertation, Oxford University, in progress.

HOOKS, N. C. "Sir John Vanbrugh: A Reevaluation of His Plays." Master's
thesis, University of Liverpool, 1955–1956. Adds little that is new to
Vanbrugh criticism.

MAYO, MARIANNE KUNERTH. "John Vanbrugh's *The Relapse*: A Study of Its
Meaning." Ph.D. dissertation, University of Florida, 1968. Examines
the philosophical and religious ideas behind Loveless's fall.

PATTERSON, FRANK M. "The Achievement of Sir John Vanbrugh." Ph.D.
dissertation, University of Iowa, 1966. Traces the stage history of each
play and includes an excellent and detailed survey of the changes made
in the translations. Vanbrugh's contributions to comedy are farce and a
new realism.

ROACH, JOSEPH. "Vanbrugh's English Baroque: Opera and the Opera House in the Haymarket." Ph.D. dissertation, Cornell University, 1973. The influence of Vanbrugh on English opera.

WEISS, SAMUEL ABBA. "Hobbism and Restoration Comedy." Ph.D. dissertation, Columbia University, 1953. Considers Vanbrugh to be a Hobbist.

3. Articles

ASHPITEL, ARTHUR. "Vanbrugh." Encyclopaedia Britannica, 8th ed. (1860), pp. 515–19. The most accurate and detailed early life; based on manuscripts in the British Museum and elsewhere and upon extensive knowledge of Vanbrugh's era.

AVERY, EMMETT L. "The Capacity of the Queen's Theater in the Haymarket." Philological Quarterly, XXXI (January 1952), 85–87. Seating totalled more than seven hundred.

BARNARD, JOHN. "Sir John Vanbrugh: Two Unpublished Letters." Huntington Library Quarterly, XXIX (1966), 347–52. First is his earliest extant letter, December 28, 1685; the second deals with opera, May 14, 1708.

BERKELEY, DAVID S. "The Art of 'Whining' Love." Studies in Philology, LII (July 1955), 478–96. This article and the two that follow show the influence of préciosité (idealized woman) on late seventeenth century comedy.

————. "The Penitent Rake in Restoration Comedy." Modern Philology, XLIX (May 1952), 223–33.

————. "Préciosité and the Restoration Comedy of Manners." Huntington Library Quarterly, XVIII (February 1955), 109–28.

BERKOWITZ, GERALD M. "Sir John Vanbrugh and the Conventions of Restoration Comedy." Genre, VI (September 1973), 346–61. Vanbrugh introduced a new realism into comedy of manners.

BIRRELL, AUGUSTINE. "Sir John Vanbrugh (1894)." In The Collected Essays and Addresses, 1880–1920, vol. I, pp. 107–12. New York: Charles Scribner's Sons, 1894; reprinted Freeport, New York: Books for Libraries Press, 1968. Post-Macaulay praise for Vanbrugh as a man of ideas.

BOYS, RICHARD C. "The Architect Vanbrugh and the Wits." College Art Journal, VI (1947), 283–90. Laughter at him was largely political.

CECIL, C. D. " 'Une espèce d'éloquence abrégée': The Idealized Speech of Restoration Comedy." Études Anglaises, XIX (1966), 15–25. Restoration comedy reflects a high degree of interest in the refinement of conversational expression.

————. "Libertine and Precieux Elements in Restoration Comedy." Essays in Criticism, IX (1959), 239–53. Restoration comedy attempts to realize an ideal personality by ridiculing extremes of refined conduct.

COLEMAN, ANTONY. "Five Notes on *The Provok'd Wife.*" *Notes and Queries*, XVI (August 1969), 298–300.

————. "Sir John Brute on the Eighteenth Century Stage." *Restoration and 18th Century Theatre Research*, VIII (November 1969), 41–46. Stage history and interpretations of Brute.

DURANT, JACK D. "*The Relapse*, Shakespeare's *Romeo*, and Otway's *Marius.*" *Restoration and 18th Century Theatre Research*, XII (November 1973), 46–49. Possible influences of Otway's Shakespearean adaptation on *The Relapse*.

FALLER, LINCOLN B. "Between Jest and Earnest: The Comedy of Sir John Vanbrugh." *Modern Philology*, LXXII (August 1974), 17–29. *The Relapse* and *The Provoked Wife* should be read as comedies that also present complex pictures of marital turmoil.

HARLEY, GRAHAM D. "*Squire Trelooby* and *The Cornish Squire:* A Reconsideration." *Philological Quarterly*, XLIX (October 1970), 520–29. Ralph's *The Cornish Squire* is plagiarized from Ozell.

HAZLITT, WILLIAM. "Lecture IV." In *Lectures on the English Comic Writers*. London: Taylor and Hessey, 1819; reprinted New York: Doubleday, Dolphin Books, n.d. The most judicious nineteenth-century estimate of the literary qualities of Vanbrugh's plays.

HODGES, JOHN C. "The Authorship of *Squire Trelooby.*" *Review of English Studies*, IV (October 1928), 404–13. Announces the discovery that the 1704 *Squire Trelooby* was included in Ozell's works (1714).

HUGHES, LEO, and A. H. SCOUTEN. "The Penzance Promptbook of *The Pilgrim.*" *Modern Philology*, LXXIII (August 1975), 33–53. Eighteenth-century revisions in Vanbrugh's translation from Fletcher attempted, unsuccessfully, to eliminate offensive passages.

HUNT, HUGH. "Restoration Acting." In *Restoration Theatre*, edited by John Russell Brown and Bernard Harris. London: Edward Arnold, 1965, pp. 179–192.

HUNT, LEIGH. "Sir John Vanbrugh." In *Sir John Vanbrugh*, edited by A. E. H. Swaen. London: T. F. Unwin, 1896; reprinted London: Ernest Benn Limited, 1949. A sketch of Vanbrugh's career, concluding that he "is easy in invention, and true and various in character" (p. 35).

HUSEBOE, ARTHUR R. " 'Lead out' in Vanbrugh's *The Provoked Wife.*" *Notes and Queries*, XXI (August 1974), 295–96. The term refers to the ceremonious escorting of a lady by a gentleman.

————. "Pope's Critical Views of the London Stage." *Restoration and 18th Century Theatre Research*, III (May 1964), 25–37. Notes the dislike of men of wit for opera.

————. "Vanbrugh: Additions to the Correspondence." *Philological Quarterly*, LIII (January 1974), 135–40. Correspondence relating to opera productions in 1708 and to the building of Kings Weston.

KERN, RONALD C. "Documents Relating to Company Management, 1705–1711." *Theatre Notebook*, XIV (Winter 1959), 60–65. New information on Vanbrugh's opera affairs.

KROPF, C. R. "*The Relapse* and the Sentimental Mask." *Journal of Narrative Technique*, I (September 1971), 193–99. The play is a twofold attack on Cibber's sentimentality.

LAMB, CHARLES. "On the Artificial Comedy of the Last Century." *The Collected Essays of Charles Lamb*, vol. I, pp. 165–72. London: J. M. Dent and Sons, 1929. An early nineteenth century effort to reevaluate Restoration comedy; it is seen as remote from real life, a "Utopia of gallantry."

LAWRENCE, W. J. "The Early Years of the First English Opera House." *The Musical Quarterly*, VII (January 1921), 104–17. Valuable for Vanbrugh's career as impresario.

MACAULAY, THOMAS BABINGTON. "Leigh Hunt: Comic Dramatists of the Restoration." In *The Miscellaneous Works of Lord Macaulay*, edited by Lady Trevelyan, vol. V, pp. 109–72. Philadelphia: The Universal Library Association, n.d. Resumes the attack on immorality in Restoration comedy.

MUESCHKE, PAUL and JEANNETTE FLEISHER. "A Re-evaluation of Vanbrugh." *Publications of the Modern Language Association*, XLIX (September 1934), 848–89. In Vanbrugh we find "a more rational and sympathetic treatment" of the problems of marriage and primogeniture.

MULLIN, DONALD C. "The Queen's Theatre, Haymarket: Vanbrugh's Opera House." *Theatre Survey*, VIII (1967), 84–105. Traces the history of the building.

OLLESON, PHILIP. "Vanbrugh and Opera at the Queen's Theatre, Haymarket." *Theatre Notebook*, XXVI (Spring 1972), 94–101. Reviews Vanbrugh's career as impresario, quoting copiously from the correspondence. Prints two previously unpublished Vanbrugh letters relating to opera affairs.

OLSHEN, BARRY N. "The Original and 'Improved' Comedies of Sir John Vanbrugh: Their Nineteenth-Century London Stage History." *Restoration and 18th Century Theatre Research*, XIII (May 1974), 27–52. Vanbrugh's nineteenth century reputation was largely based on adapted versions of his plays.

PATTERSON, FRANK M. "The Revised Scenes of *The Provok'd Wife*." *English Language Notes*, IV (September 1966), 19–23. Original scenes and revised were performed during the same period.

PETERSON, WILLIAM M. "Cibber's *She Wou'd, and She Wou'd Not* and Vanbrugh's *Aesop*." *Philological Quarterly*, XXXV (October 1956), 429–35. Cibber borrowed and enlarged.

ROBERTS, PHILIP. "Vanbrugh's Lost Play: The Prologue." *Restoration and*

18th Century Theatre Research, XII (May 1973), 57–58. Prints the previously unpublished prologue to *The Cuckold in Conceit*.

ROPER, ALAN. "Language and Action in *The Way of the World, Love's Last Shift*, and *The Relapse*." *ELH*, XL (Spring 1973), 44–69. The satirical vitality of language in *The Relapse* contributes to Vanbrugh's picture of social decay.

ROSENBERG, ALBERT. "New Light on Vanbrugh." *Philological Quarterly*, XLV (July 1966), 603–13. Prints his earliest letter (December 28, 1685) and a new letter from the Bastille (August 26, 1692).

SCOUTEN, A. H. "Notes Toward a History of Restoration Comedy." *Philological Quarterly*, XLV (January 1966), 62–70. Notes that Southerne's *The Wives Excuse* (December 1691) displays the shift of attention in comedy of manners from the "gay couple" to the problems of the married couple.

SECCOMBE, THOMAS. "Sir John Vanbrugh." In *The Dictionary of National Biography*. Edited by Leslie Stephen and Sidney Lee, vol XX. London: Oxford University Press, 1921–1922. Useful summary of known facts about Vanbrugh's life and career.

SHEPPARD, F. H. W., gen. ed. "The Haymarket Opera House." In *Survey of London*, vol. XXIX, ch. VIII, pp. 223–50. London: Athlone Press, University of London, for the London County Council, 1960. Provides essential details of land acquisition and construction of the first eighteenth century London theater. Notes to the chapter are in vol. XXX, pp. 568–72.

SHERWOOD, IRMA Z. "Vanbrugh's 'Romeo and Juliet': A Note on *The Relapse*." *Restoration and 18th Century Theatre Research*, XII (November 1973), 41–45. There are hints of the Fashion-Hoyden plot in Shakespeare and in Otway's *Caius Marius*.

SHIPLEY, JOHN B. "The Authorship of *The Cornish Squire*." *Philological Quarterly*, XLVII (April 1968), 145–56. Represents the Vanbrugh-Congreve-Walsh collaboration.

THAYLER, ALWIN. "Sir John Vanbrugh: *The Provok'd Wife*—Critical Essay." In *Dryden and His Contemporaries*, vol. IV of *Representative English Comedies*, edited by Charles Mills Gayley and Alwin Thaler, pp. 407–26. New York: Macmillan, 1936. Concise and sound introduction to Vanbrugh's works and to *The Provok'd Wife*.

VAN NIEL, PIETER JAN. "*The Relapse*—Into Death and Damnation." *Educational Theatre Journal*, XXI (October 1969), 318–32. The play is a powerful picture of pessimism.

WEBB, GEOFFREY. "Sir John Vanbrugh." *Burlington Magazine*, XLVII (November 1925), 222–27. Vanbrugh's Romantic character led to his experiments in Gothic architecture.

Index

(The works of Vanbrugh are listed under his name)

Addison, Joseph, 57, 85, 107, 156n85;
  Rosamond, 57, 58; *The Spectator*, 68,
  107, 156n85
Aesop at Bath, 36
Aesop at Epsom, 36
Alleman, Gellert S., 72, 114
Anglicans, 19
Anne, Queen, 39, 48, 51, 52, 59
Ashley, Leonard, 68
Assassination Plot, The, 39
Avery, Emmett L., 52–53

Baker, David, 142
Barques, de, 131
Barry Elizabeth, 37
Behn, Aphra, 68, 86
Berkeley, Baron. *See* John Berkeley
Berkeley, John, 27, 38
Bertie family, 24
Bertillier, Mr., 25
Betterton, Thomas, 32, 33, 35–37, 41,
  42, 44, 45, 47, 48, 50–55, 100, 102,
  116, 119, 151n7
Bicknell, Mrs. Mary, 131
Birrell, Augustine, 108, 145
Bishop of London, 20
Blenheim Palace, 18, 50–51, 54, 57, 58
Board of Works, 47
Bodleian library (Oxford), 20
Bononcini, Giovanni, 131
Boursault, Édme, 35, 116–19, 161n2;
  Les Fables d'Ésope, 35, 116, 118, 119
Bowen, William, 58
Bracegirdle, Anne, 37, 50, 127
Brett, Colonel Henry, 58, 59, 155n77

Briscoe, Samuel, 39
Brown, Tom, 46
Bruce, Mrs., 131
Bull, John, 52
Bullock, Christopher, 56
Burke, Edmund, 143

Carberry, Lord. *See* John Vaughn
Carleton, Baron. *See* Sir Dudley Carle-
  ton (elder)
Carleton, Sir Dudley (elder), 19
Carleton, Sir Dudley, 19, 20
Carlisle, Earl of. *See* Charles Howard
Carlisle Herald Extraordinary, 48
Carlyle, Thomas, 108
Carmarthen, Marquis of. *See* Peregrine
  Osborne
Castle Howard, 17, 18, 44, 46–48, 50,
  58, 147
Cat, Christopher, 43
Centlivre, Susanna, 68
Charles I, 21
Charles II, 28–29
Chaucer, Geoffrey, 40, 99; "The
  Franklin's Tale," 98
Chester (Cheshire), 20–22
"Chevy Chase," 110
Churchill, John, 48, 50, 55, 57, 59, 134
Cibber, Colley, 17, 27, 32–37, 40, 47,
  48, 50, 53, 56–58, 61–69, 77, 79, 80,
  82–84, 86, 100, 111, 117, 119, 133–43,
  149n1, 156n2; *An Apology for the Life
  of Colley Cibber*, 27, 36, 58, 142,
  149n1; *The Careless Husband*, 84,
  111; *Love's Last Shift: or The Fool in*

Fashion, 32, 33, 35, 62–69, 78, 80, 83, 86; *The Provok'd Husband,* 62, 133–41
Civilisation, 134
Clarenceux King at Arms, 17, 18, 50
Clarendon, Earl of (Lord Lieutenant of Ireland), 22, 23
Clayton, Thomas, 59, 60; *Arsinoe, Queen of Cyprus,* 32, 52
Coke, Thomas, 59, 60
Collier, Jeremy, 30, 31, 37–41, 69, 73, 81, 87–89, 111–13, 124, 141, 143, 152n27; *A Short View of the Immorality and Profaneness of the English Stage,* 30–31, 38, 39
Comédie Française, 35, 37
Comparison Between the Two Stages, A, 35, 123
Congreve, William, 18, 30–33, 36, 37, 39, 42, 44, 48–54, 56, 63, 66, 68, 77, 84, 87, 88, 91, 94, 95, 101, 107, 110, 137, 142–46; "Amendments of Mr. Collier's False and Imperfect Citations," 39; *The Double Dealer,* 39, 110; *Love for Love,* 31, 33, 36, 86, 87, 108; *The Mourning Bride,* 37; *The Old Batchelor,* 36, 44, 101, 107; *The Way of the World,* 30, 42, 66, 67, 73, 94, 101, 105, 110
Consultation, The, 54
Cooper, The Reverend John, 46
Covent Garden Theatre, 57
Croissant, De Witt C., 68
Cumberland, Richard, 134

Daily Courant, 40, 49, 58
Dancourt, Florent-Carton, 37, 55, 74, 117, 120, 125; *Les Bourgeoises à la Mode,* 55, 117, 125–126; *La Maison de Campagne,* 37, 117, 120
Davenant, Sir William, 31, 36; *The Siege of Rhodes,* 31
Davies, Thomas, 62, 142
Defoe, Daniel, 109
Dennis, John, 29, 84, 90, 156n85
Dibdin, Charles, 142
Dieupart, Charles, 52
Dilke, Thomas, 86; *The Lover's Luck,* 86
Disraili, Isaac, 149n1
Diverting Post, 51

Dobrée, Bonamy, 46, 63–64, 91
Dodington, George Bubb, 134
Doggett, Thomas, 33, 50, 61, 117
Donne, John: "The Funeral," 105
Dorchester, Viscount. *See* Sir Dudley Carleton (elder)
Dorset Garden Theatre, 42, 56
Dorset, Lord. *See* Charles Sackville
Downes, John, 52, 131, 155n65
Drury Lane Theatre, 31–35, 41, 42, 46, 52, 53, 55–63, 117, 119, 137
Dryden, John, 31, 42, 44–46, 109, 117, 121, 146; *The Fables,* 44; *Marriage à la Mode,* 109–110; *The Spanish Friar,* 146
D'Urfey, Thomas, 35, 39, 46, 56, 68, 87, 88; *Cinthia and Endimion,* 35; *Don Quixote,* 39, 87–88; *Wonders in the Sun,* 56

Elford, Mrs., 131
Eliot, T. S., 90
Etherege, Sir George, 29, 30, 68, 74, 91, 92, 94, 95, 101, 142, 143, 145, 146; *The Man of Mode, or, Sir Fopling Flutter,* 30, 80, 83, 92; *She Wou'd if She Cou'd,* 73–74, 95, 101, 105
Evelyn, John, 151n10

Farquhar, George, 42, 68, 143–46; *The Constant Couple,* 42; *The Stratagem,* 58
Fielding, Henry, 143; *Pasquin,* 143; *Tom Jones,* 134, 143
Finch, Daniel, 25, 26, 150n4, 150n17
Finger, Gottfried, 45
First Churchills, The, 134
Fleisher, Jeannette, 64, 80, 98, 114
Fletcher, John, 42, 45, 116, 117, 121, 122; *The Pilgrim,* 42, 45, 116, 117, 121
Fone, B. R. S., 68
Friend, Sir John, 38, 40

Garrick, David, 35–36, 100, 102; *Lethe: or Esop in the Shades,* 35–36
Garth, Dr. Samuel, 46, 48, 54, 153n44
Gay, John, 156n85; *The Beggar's Opera,* 62, 126, 156n85
George I, 17, 57

George of Hanover, Prince. *See* George
  I
Gildon, Charles, 35, 142, 156n85
Glorious Revolution, 25, 26, 43
Goddard, Mr., 25
Goldsmith, Oliver, 18, 143, 145
Gosse, Sir Edmund, 49
Granville, George, 55, 58, 86; *The*
  British Enchanters, 55, 58
Gray, Thomas, 68
Greber, Giacome, 52; *The Loves of Er-*
  gasto, 52–54
Grimaldi, Nicolino, 60, 61
Grisoni, Giuseppi, 17

Haines, Joe, 33, 41
Halifax, Baron (later Earl of Halifax). *See*
  Charles Montague (1661–1715)
Handel, George Frederick, 61; *Rinaldo*,
  61
Harley, Graham D., 50
Hastings, Theophilus, 22, 23, 44,
  150n10
Haym, Nicolino, 52, 56, 60; *Camilla*, 55;
  Pyrrhus and Demetrius, 60
Haymarket Theatre. *See* Queen's
  Theatre
Hazlitt, William, 82, 87, 102, 111, 125,
  133, 141, 143
Heidegger, John James, 61
Henry II, 57
Henry, Matthew, 21
Hinton, Edward, 46
Hobbes, Thomas, 76, 101
Hodges, John C., 50
Holford, Thomas, 47–48
Holles, John, 61, 154n49
Hotson, Leslie, 37
Howard, Charles, 23, 44, 47, 50, 61,
  153n40
Hunt, Leigh, 133, 141, 144
Huntingdon (also Huntington), Earl of.
  See Theophilus Hastings

Ibsen, Henrik, 92

Jacob, Giles, 142
James I, 19
James II, 21, 23, 24, 39

Jennings, Sarah, 18, 54, 134
Johnson, Samuel, 110, 141; *The Lives of*
  the Poets, 141
Jonson, Ben, 68, 142, 143; *Volpone*, 57

Keally, Joseph, 48, 56
Kent, Marquis of, 57, 59, 61
Kent, Mrs. Mary, 33
Killigrew, Thomas, 36
King's School (Chester), 21
King's Theatre. *See* Queen's Theatre
Kingston, Earl of, 42, 43
Kit-Cat Club, 17, 23, 41–49, 54, 57, 58
Kneller, Sir Godfrey, 17, 44, 149n1,
  153n38
Knights of the Toast, 42
Krutch, Joseph Wood, 39

Lagny, M. l'abbé, 25
Lamb, Charles, 133, 141, 143
Laureat, The, 39
Lee, Nathaniel: *Caesar Borgia*, 34
Leeds, Duchess of, 137
Lesage, Alain René, 46, 117, 123; *Le*
  Traître Puni, 46, 117, 123
L'Estrange, Roger, 142
Lincoln's Inn Fields Theatre, 31–33, 36,
  37, 41, 42, 44, 49, 50, 53, 54, 62, 86,
  119
Lock Up Your Daughters, 134
Locke, John 93
Lodi, Anna, 59
Lord Chamberlain. *See* Marquis of Kent
Louis XIV, 24, 26–27
Louvoirs, Mr. de, 24
Luttrell, Narcissus, 39

Macaulay, Thomas Babington, 136, 144,
  145
MacCarthy, Owen, 22
Macklin, Charles, 100
Mainwaring, Alderman, 21
Mainwaring, Arthur, 54, 155n69
Manchester, Earl of. *See* Charles Mon-
  tagu (1660–1722)
Manchester, Lady 144
Mandeville, Bernard, 36; *The Fable of*
  the Bees, 36; *Some Fables after. . . La*
  Fontaine, 36

Vanbrugh, Giles (grandfather), 19
Vanbrugh, Lady Henrietta, 115, 141
Vanbrugh, Mary (grandmother), 19
Vanbrugh, William (uncle), 19
Vanbrugh, William (cousin), 26
Vanbrugh, Sir John: active in the Kit-Cat
  Club, 41–50; ancestry, 18–20; ap-
  pointed auditor, 26–27; appointed
  Carlisle Herald Extraordinary, 48; as-
  signs plays to Drury Lane and operas

ceit, 58; writes *The Pilgrim* to benefit
  Dryden, 45–46; writes *The Provok'd*
  Wife, 27, 36; writes *The Relapse*,
  32–33, 63; writes "A Short Vindication," 39

WORKS: DRAMA
Aesop I, 35, 36, 89, 116, 117, *118–20*,
  121, 129, 131, 135, 137, 161n2

Marlborough, Duchess of. *See* Sarah Jennings

Marlborough, Duke of. *See* John Churchill

Mary, Queen, 29, 35

Meredith, George, 144; "An Essay on Comedy," 144

Meriton, John, 18

Perils of Pauline, The, 63

Perkins, Sir William, 39, 40

Pontchartrain (minister to Louis XIV), 24

Pope, Alexander, 34, 88, 141, 142, 156n85; "The Rape of the Lock," 105

Popish Plot, 20

Porter, Mary, 137